SENATE
STREET & SAVORY

Daniel Wright

with
**COURTNEY TSITOURIS
& DONNA COVRETT**

Photography by **ANTHONY TAHLIER**

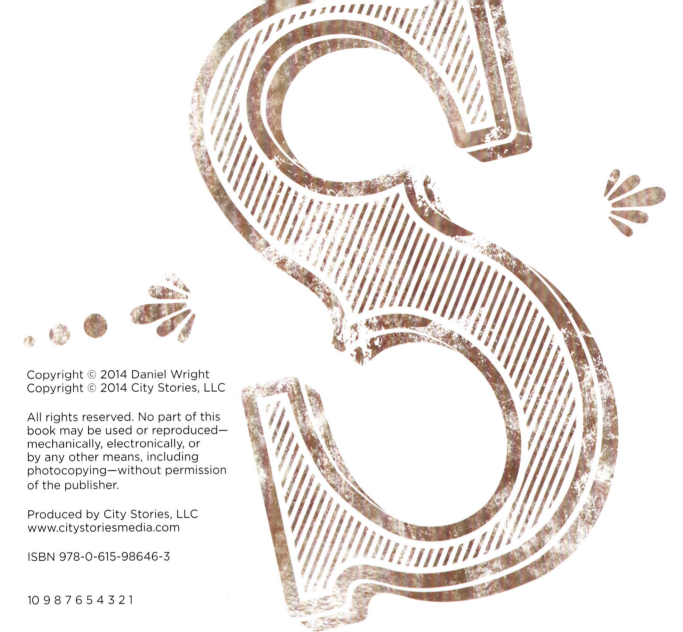

Copyright © 2014 Daniel Wright
Copyright © 2014 City Stories, LLC

All rights reserved. No part of this book may be used or reproduced—mechanically, electronically, or by any other means, including photocopying—without permission of the publisher.

Produced by City Stories, LLC
www.citystoriesmedia.com

ISBN 978-0-615-98646-3

10 9 8 7 6 5 4 3 2 1

Written & edited by
Courtney Tsitouris
& Donna Covrett

Photography by Anthony Tahlier
except pages 37, 39, 64, 66, 86, 127 by Anna Penny,
pages 39, 97, 110, 152, 163 by Chris Smith,
and page 21 by Leah Brady

Book design by Kelly Pennington

Illustrations by Dave Rickerd

Proofreading & indexing by Stephanie Meinberg

Printed in the U.S.A.

FOR
KNOX & OLIVER

CONTENTS

FOREWORD — 7

HOW TO USE THIS BOOK — 8
Birth Wright — 11
Firecracker — 18

SIDEKICKS — 22
Some Sort of Magic — 36
Notes from a Retired Line Cook — 39
Underdogs — 44
Duck Fat Deal — 48

DOGS — 50
Haute Dog — 52
Sleep When We Die — 65
Kitchen Wisdom — 67
Going to See a Man About a Dog — 73
Family Matters — 110

STREET & SAVORY — 120
War Room with Friends — 126
Farmer Sallie — 137
Turning Tables — 153
Street Fight — 162

ENCASED MEAT — 170

PANTRY — 174

COCKTAILS — 192
It's Personal — 211

THANKS — 218

INDEX — 220

FOREWORD

⋯⇒ Courtney Tsitouris ⇐⋯

WITH HIS MANICURED beard and wave of red hair, Dan Wright is part mountain man, part surfer boy, part Conan O'Brien. And yet it's his tenacity and entrepreneurial spirit that make him more like New York restaurateur Danny Meyer—known for opening exactly the right kind of restaurants at exactly the right times.

For the past four years, I've watched Dan light up the Cincinnati restaurant scene with an unusual brand of swagger and sartorial style. In 2010, his upscale hot dog concept at Senate thundered through Cincinnati's Over-the-Rhine neighborhood, converting even the most dispassionate dog lovers into hard-core evangelists. Two more restaurants followed suit—Abigail Street and Pontiac—both of them with a distinct sense of place and culinary perspective.

By 2012, I was convinced that Dan's prowess as a chef and restaurateur would lead him to national acclaim (I was right—later that year he was named *Food & Wine* magazine's People's Best New Chef, Great Lakes) That's about the time I started calling, emailing, and texting him incessantly about publishing a Senate cookbook. As a writer, few creative endeavors had ever been this juicy, and far fewer had smash-hit potential. I was dying to make it happen.

It was a gusty evening in late December when I finally pinned Dan down for a talk. We tucked ourselves in at a low-lit bar with a flight of bourbon sippers and agreed to create the kind of cookbook we'd always wanted to read.

SO WHAT EXACTLY is Senate like? Walk inside and find an archetype of urban cool—lipsticked chic-sters and bow-tied hipsters sitting elbow-to-elbow, framed by exposed brick and polished concrete. The space thrums as service staff weaves in and out of the crowd delivering badass dogs and street food.

For me, it all started with Mussels Charmoula, with its kicky, saffron-hued sauce. Next was the slyly named Trailer Park hot dog buried beneath a drift of coleslaw and crushed barbecue chips. The homespun comfort of poutine—a stack of short ribs, gravy, and duck fat fries—sealed the deal.

Pretty amazing considering its location in a neighborhood that had long been neglected. As Dan and his wife Lana prepped for the opening of Senate, their view out onto Vine Street was a fairly bleak one, with a few quiet storefronts and a lone bistro across the way. Today—with dozens of new businesses and residential developments—you are lucky to find a place to park. In its fifty-five-seat room, Senate feeds 1,200 diners a week, each of them perfectly willing to wait hours to score a table.

DURING THE PROCESS of making this book, I've spent a lot of time with Dan and his inner circle. I've had intimate and weird conversations. Heard things I can't unhear, seen things I can't unsee—most notably the bar manager's bare ass as he posed for a photo with a Christmas reindeer. But never mind that. What I've discovered is that the Senate crew is a rarified breed of brash, talented, and highly creative goofballs who behave more like family than anything else. The by-product of their alliance is what you see squeezed between these covers—deceptively simple food you might not think to create for yourself.

So here it is: the tale of how Senate came to be, a behind-the-scenes peek into one of the quirkiest and most dynamic restaurants in the country, with over 160 recipes you can actually make, and one of my proudest collaborations to date. Whether you dive into the lobster BLT or one of the thirty-plus dogs, I highly recommend including some friends and cracking open a couple of cold ones. Just make sure to have plenty of napkins. You're going to need them.

CWT, 2014

HOW TO USE THIS BOOK

We're all about component cooking at Senate. We've got a TON OF CONDIMENTS on hand at any given time and we use them in a variety of ways. YOU CAN DO THE SAME. Say a recipe in this book calls for our spicy peanut sauce (page 63). You may prefer something sweeter, so you might choose the brown sugar peanut sauce (page 185) instead. Or maybe you don't eat pork. You can easily swap it for lamb or beef. We've made these kinds of substitutions easy by providing TIPS AND RECOMMENDATIONS along the way. We also have a few workhorse recipes we use repeatedly—like braised beef short ribs (page 166), braised pork belly (page 168), and foie gras torchon (page 140). Once you've got them mastered, THE SKY'S THE LIMIT as far as cooking goes. So remember to change things up and have fun. By all means, personalize these recipes and MAKE THEM YOUR OWN. We've left plenty of room to take notes. Whatever you do, don't settle for plain ketchup.

THE BASICS

BUTTER
We always use unsalted butter for cooking. It allows you to season the dish as you cook, controlling the flavor as well as the amount of sodium. Plus, since salt acts as a preservative to provide a longer shelf life, unsalted butter is usually fresher.

OLIVE OIL
Olive oil is great for sautéing because it has a higher smoke point—which means you can get your pans hotter for a good sear. Extra virgin olive oil is best for emulsifying vinaigrettes for a rich, creamy finish.

SALT & PEPPER
Kosher salt, period. The grains are bigger than table salt, which makes them easier to pinch with your fingers and control the seasoning. Pepper means whole peppercorns, freshly ground for superior flavor.

STOCK
At Senate, we make our own stocks with beef and veal bones. If you're going to purchase stock at the market, make sure to get a product that's low in sodium.

HOT DOGS
All beef, baby. We have our dogs made locally by Avril-Bleh & Sons Meat Market, but there are a variety of store brands we strongly recommend. On the East Coast, there's Nathan's and Hebrew National, which have a lot more garlic. In the Midwest, Vienna Beef and Bobak's products are great. Farmer John dogs are readily available on the West Coast. Even if you can't find some of these brands in your area, you can always have them shipped to your doorstep. Life's too short to eat bad hot dogs.

BUNS
For hot dogs and burgers, we prefer egg buns. They're rich, fluffy, and have a lot of flavor. Because they're not as dense as other varieties, they also toast up nicely. At Senate, we use buns from Giminetti Baking Company, a Cincinnati favorite. Wonder Bread egg buns work great too. In the words of Sir Mix-A-Lot, "My anaconda don't want none unless you've got buns, hun."

BACON
This book calls for mostly applewood smoked or black pepper bacon. Go to the market or your local butcher and get the fresh stuff, which means bacon that's in the display case instead of sealed in Cryovac. Don't go cheap. There's only so much you can eat in life, so you might as well get the best.

RENDERED FAT
Whenever we're cooking off bacon or any other kind of pork product, we reserve the fat in a jar and store it in the fridge. It lasts for months, and it's delicious for sautés as well as drizzled over warm fries (page 24).

HERBS
All the recipes in this book call for fresh herbs. Make sure to store them in an upright position—the same way they're actually grown. If you want to try growing fresh herbs, start with thyme. It grows year-round and survives really cold and crappy weather.

SRIRACHA
Sriracha is a hot sauce made from ground chili peppers, vinegar, and garlic. It adds a nice amount of spice and salt to whatever you're cooking. Our favorite variety is made by Huy Fong, which you can buy pretty much anywhere.

COOKWARE
We recommend nonreactive cookware: ceramic-coated cast iron and stainless steel in pots and pans; mixing bowls made from glass, stainless steel, or plastic. Try to stay away from aluminum cookware, because it reacts with highly acidic food and leaves a weird metallic taste.

SAUSAGE STUFFERS & GRINDERS
If you are not interested in investing the big bucks in a professional sausage stuffer or grinder, that's okay. KitchenAid makes some really great attachments for your stand mixer that work just as well and are a lot more economical.

BIRTH WRIGHT

Senate opened on February 19, 2010, and yet the story hardly begins there. It starts in Chicago with my mom and dad who separated when I was eight years old, mostly because my mom wouldn't tolerate any of his shit.

My dad had this little Cessna plane and he'd fly his girlfriends up to Wisconsin where my grandfather owned a farm. He wouldn't come home for days on end, which increasingly got under my mom's skin. One day she called the airport, learned that the plane was logged out, and decided to take action. When my dad flew home a few days later, he looked out the cockpit window to see the word "pig" mowed into our front lawn.

Not long after that I heard them both screaming upstairs. "Don't be a coward!" my mom yelled. "If you're going to go, then you need to tell the boys." A couple days later, he was gone.

After the split, my mom went to work full time at a large corporate bank. She started as a receptionist and eventually became an account manager in charge of multibillion dollar accounts. She'd get up at six in the morning, take the train into the city, and work until late in the evening. Hustling that much as a single mother was a hard gig, but I loved her for it. When she'd call and ask me to take something out of the freezer for dinner, I was happy to help out. That's pretty much how I started cooking. I'm not saying I was any good at it, but I loved doing it, and it became routine for me to put dinner on the table for my mother and my brother, Chris, every night.

Cooking wasn't considered a very masculine thing to do, especially if you asked my father. He was a strict, rigid thinker, in part because he was born into a military family. By the time he was twenty-one, he had already served two tours in Vietnam. While stationed in Khe Sanh, his job was to take soldiers off helicopters after they had returned from battle—whether they were alive or dead. All the while, he'd be getting shot at with napalm exploding around him.

When he came back to the states, he married my mom. A couple years later, they lost their first-born child, my older brother who I never knew. Soon after, my father's mother died. By the time I came along, he'd experienced so much death that he had become a master of cutting himself off from other people.

After my parents got divorced, I wasn't the best student and routinely got poor grades. Not having my pops in the house had a huge impact on my attitude. I fought constantly with authority and mouthed off to anyone who tried to tell me what the fuck to do, including my mom and teachers.

My dad stationed in Khe Sanh during the Vietnam war.

But that would soon change. Surprisingly, I made it out of high school in one piece. With my love of food still intact, I enrolled in culinary school at Johnson & Wales in Rhode Island.

My first internship was at a big chain hotel where I spent most of my time piping mashed potatoes on plates and serving food from a giant conveyer belt. I hated the artificiality. The semester before graduation, I dropped out of school to find work at a real restaurant. This sent both my parents over the edge, especially my father. To him, the only thing worse than pursuing a career in the kitchen was quitting something I'd started. Our relationship became even more bruised and volatile, but I didn't care. I was still dumb enough to think I had all the answers.

Three days later, I landed my first real gig in Chicago at Spago working for Wolfgang Puck. Problem was, I was an immature little punk and couldn't handle that my buddies were out partying nights and weekends. After the third or fourth time I cut out of work early to meet them, my boss just looked at me and said, "You gotta go, kid." So, I did.

Soon after, I walked into Gordon, Chicago's longest standing four-star restaurant, and was hired on the spot. I wound up as an apprentice to this cook named Miguel who was 5' 2" and the meanest and fastest little fucker I'd ever met. When I plated a dish that wasn't good enough, he'd slide it back and tell me to do it over. Every night by the end of my shift, I wanted to cry. Meanwhile my boss, Don, was trying to teach me how to buckle down. "Do you want to be like your dipshit friends, or do you want to make something of yourself?" He made a good point. I spent the next two years putting my head down, learning everything I could about the restaurant industry from the back of the house to the front. At Gordon, I finally found the discipline and structure I had been searching for all along. After two years, I was eager to test myself somewhere else.

That's when I made the move to Blackbird to work with Paul Kahan, who would soon grace the cover of *Food & Wine* magazine as one of their Best New Chefs. About a week after he received the title, one of our pantry cooks knocked a

knife off of the counter, sending it point-down through the top of Paul's shoe and into his foot. For weeks he hobbled around autographing the "Best New Chefs" issue. That was Paul though. He never lost his cool, and I admired the hell out of him for it. I'll never forget the night he said to me, "Look, you need to relax. You're going to go as far as you want to go, but you need to be patient." He was a brilliant coach.

Even so, I was restless. Desperate to make a bigger name for myself, I moved to Los Angeles to take an executive chef position at a bistro called Boxer. It was about the same time that my dad started getting sick. At only fifty-one, he was diagnosed with neuropathy, a nerve disease that would eventually leave him numb from the legs down. Maybe the news of his illness softened him, or maybe it was all the miles between us—I don't know. For whatever reason, he started calling me, and we began talking pretty regularly.

After two years, I was burnt out on L.A. and moved back to Chicago to be closer to my family. I took a job at a Middle Eastern restaurant called Souk. That's where I met Lana, this little firecracker from Cincinnati who was hired as a server. There were sparks between us immediately, and somehow I knew she was going to change my life. It wasn't long before we were dating and traveling to Cincinnati to visit her family. In the meantime, I was starting to think about building a restaurant of my own. Lana and I spent a lot of time walking around downtown Cincinnati and looking through windows at abandoned spaces. The city felt like a smaller version of Chicago but without the oversaturated dining scene. We decided that if a new concept was going to work anywhere, Cincinnati was the place.

I couldn't believe I had found a girl who loved me and loved the restaurant business so much. Lana inspired me to stay focused and never forget my dreams. In 2007, we packed our things and moved. We were ready to take the plunge together.

The next two years were the hardest and scariest years of our lives. The process of opening Senate emptied our bank accounts and frazzled our nerves. I'd lie in bed every night and feel fucking terrible for putting Lana through the stress, for risking everything we had on an idea that wasn't even guaranteed to work. In the meantime, my father kept me grounded. We'd talk at least once a day, and some days up to four or five times. As a retired foreman, he coached me through the phases of Senate's construction. Even as his illness escalated, his enthusiasm remained solid.

When Lana and I finally opened Senate, it was to a crowd that poured in nonstop for three days. The merciless pace had us lost in a sort of fugue state. We were stressed yet relieved. Slaphappy. Buzzed. But on February 23rd—when Senate was just four days old—the bottom dropped. My father had died.

I was devastated. We closed the restaurant immediately and drove up to Wisconsin to be with my family. For weeks after, we received flowers and cards, not knowing if they were meant to congratulate us on Senate's opening or console us about our loss. What we did know, unequivocally, was that my father had held on just long enough to see Senate open. There was no coincidence about his timing.

It had taken the better part of thirty years to find our common ground, to reach an understanding that validated me not only as his son, but as a man. When he died, my father was one of my most trusted advisors, my most passionate cheerleaders. I still remember the last words he said to me: "I'm tired, and it sounds like you're tired too. I'm really proud of you. We'll talk later." But later never came, and it still pisses me off.

t DREAMS

"Don't forget dreams," a note Lana wrote to me as a reminder during hard times.

FIRECRACKER

BY LANA WRIGHT

One of the first things I noticed about Dan was the word "Scorpio" tattooed in Arabic on his right arm. Scorpios are known for being confident and intense; unafraid to ruffle feathers. I should know. I'm one too.

We met in Chicago at a Middle Eastern restaurant called Souk where I was a server and Dan was the head chef. I had just moved from Cincinnati after a bad breakup and was ready for a fresh start. Dan was one of the first people I met in the city. I thought he was incredibly obnoxious.

One night, I returned a meat dish to him because a customer had complained that it was undercooked. Dan grabbed the whole plate out of my hands, threw it in the garbage, and said, "Now they can wait!" I replied, "I'll go back there and cook it myself!" And he screamed back, "The fuck you will!" I wasn't about to take his shit.

I had grown up in the restaurant industry and wasn't about to be pushed around. Throughout the 1980s, my father and his brother owned and operated several Gold Star Chili restaurants in Cincinnati. Some of my earliest memories are of shredding cheese on a box grater while my grandma stirred chili and my dad worked at the steam table. Eventually, when I was old enough to work, I waited tables at a restaurant near my high school. I applied the same work ethic I'd seen in my dad all those years, and it paid off.

I was good at what I did. I could scan an entire dining room and quickly determine who needed a bill, who needed a drink, who wanted to chat, and who wanted to be left alone. I spent the next seven years serving or managing at several Cincinnati restaurants. At times I debated pursuing another career, but I always came back to the restaurant business. It was in my blood.

By the time I started at Souk, I was experienced and adamant about the way the dining room should be serviced. I also knew a good chef from a bad one. Dan was an amazing one, which I found annoyingly attractive. As much as I wanted to write him off as a hothead, there was something about him that fascinated me. He was smart. He knew his shit in the kitchen. There were times I even found him charming. For the longest while I couldn't figure out if I hated him or loved him.

After a year and a half, I was promoted to front of the house manager. That's when everything changed for Dan and me. We were forced to spend a lot of time together doing payroll, managing inventory, and running the restaurant.

At first, I insisted *you keep your ground, and I'll keep mine*. But that didn't last. There was an undeniable intensity and chemistry between us. Friction and passion are funny that way. You can't have one without the other, and we had plenty of both to spare. Before we knew it, we were in love and spending all our free time together.

In the meantime, business at Souk was better than ever. Dan and I had become more than best friends—we were amazing business partners. One day he looked at me and said, "We can either keep working for other people to build their dream, or we can make our own. We have what it takes to run our own place." I was scared, but I knew he was right.

In 2007, we moved to Cincinnati to start working on our own restaurant. I got a job serving at a place downtown while Dan tended bar and started the process of raising money. Meanwhile, even though we were just barely scraping by, we decided to get married. People thought we were crazy for planning a wedding during the chaos of building a restaurant, but it just felt right. Working separate jobs was the hardest part of moving to Cincinnati. Planning something big together was easy, even if we did battle it out a few times.

Sure, we could have settled for a boring relationship. We've both had plenty of that type, where everything is great and there are never any disagreements. But both of us like being challenged. Both of us would rather be with someone who presses our buttons and calls us out on our shit. If you're not fighting and passionate, then it's not worth it. That's just who we are.

Dan and me at home with our twin sons Knox and Oliver.

FRIES

SERVES 6 – 8

CHEF TIP
I prefer Kennebec potatoes because of their lower sugar content, but Yukon Gold works well, too.

6 large potatoes, peeled and cut lengthwise into ½" thick batons
1 quart vegetable oil or shortening
salt to taste

Soak potato batons in cold water. Meanwhile, in a large pot, heat oil to 350 degrees. Once hot, drain potatoes from water and pat thoroughly dry with paper towels. Place half of the potatoes in the hot oil slowly and carefully. Cook for 4 minutes. Remove and place on paper towels. Bring oil back up to temperature and repeat with other the other half. Refrigerate until ready to finish.

When ready to serve: Bring same pot of oil back to 350 degrees. Add all of the fries. Cook for 4 – 5 minutes, or until crispy. Remove from oil. Place in a bowl and toss with salt.

VARIATIONS

TRUFFLE FRIES
2 oz. truffle oil
several sprigs of thyme, leaves removed

Toss hot fries with truffle oil and thyme.

BACON FAT FRIES
2 oz. rendered bacon fat
1 or 2 pieces crisp bacon, minced
several sprigs of thyme, leaves removed

Toss hot fries with bacon fat, bacon, and thyme.

DUCK FAT FRIES
4 oz. duck fat
2 sprigs rosemary, leaves removed

Substitute duck fat for 4 ounces of vegetable oil or shortening in recipe. Toss hot fries with rosemary.

HOMEMADE PICKLES

It only takes a week to cure pickles. Eat them alone as a snack or on our Senate burger (page 160), lamb burger (page 155), or Booty & Belly sandwich (page 156). Make sure to start with pickling cukes. They're different from thick-skinned salad cucumbers, because they're picked from the vine at a younger age. They can be impossible to find in supermarkets, but you can easily wrangle them down at farm stands during the summer.

YIELD: ENOUGH FOR 3 – 4 16 OZ. JARS

CHEF TIP
Vinegar will react to aluminum, so be sure to use a stainless steel pot to heat the vinegar.

2 lb. pickling cukes, sliced into ½" rounds
1 yellow onion, thinly sliced
¾ cup kosher salt
1 ½ cups sugar
3 cups white vinegar
1 tsp. ground turmeric
3 T. mustard seeds
2 T. coriander
1 tsp. celery seed
2 T. garlic, chopped

Divide cucumber slices among 3 glass 16-ounce jars. In a pot over a medium heat, bring rest of the ingredients to a boil. Ladle pickling spice over cucumbers. Seal tightly. Turn upside down for 20 seconds to distribute pickling spices. Store in a cool, dry place. Best after a week, but can be aged for up to 6 months.

COUNTRY FRIED BACON

Inspired by Southern-style chicken-fried steak, we take a thick cut of bacon, coat it in egg wash, bread it, and fry it in hot oil. This recipe calls for rosemary, but you can also rock it with fresh thyme or oregano. Serve it alone or turn it into breakfast bliss with a fried egg and some country gravy (page 184).

SERVES 4

CHEF TIP

When you're breading anything, always keep one hand wet and one hand dry. This will help you avoid clumpy breading. It will also keep the counter clean.

1 quart vegetable oil or shortening
2 eggs + ¼ cup water for egg wash
2 cups all-purpose flour
2 sprigs rosemary, leaves removed and finely chopped
salt & pepper to taste
10 – 12 strips applewood smoked bacon
2 cups panko bread crumbs, run through food processor

In a 2-quart pot, heat oil or shortening to 350 degrees. In a bowl, combine flour, rosemary, salt and pepper. Dip each piece of bacon into egg wash, then toss into seasoned flour. Dip in egg wash a second time, then bread crumbs. Carefully add to hot oil. Fry until golden brown, about 3 minutes. Remove and drain on a paper towel-lined plate. Season with salt.

CRISPY FRIED PICKLES

We make our own pickles (page 27), but a quality grocery store brand will work for this recipe. We prefer bread and butter pickles because we like the combination of sweet, salty, and hot.

SERVES 2

CHEF TIP
You can serve these with buttermilk tarragon dressing (page 176) or beer cheese (page 185), but they're pretty much good with anything.

1 quart vegetable oil or shortening

2 eggs + ¼ cup water for egg wash

1 lb. homemade pickles (page 27) or quality pickles, sliced

2 cups panko bread crumbs

salt & pepper to taste

In a 2-quart pot, heat oil or shortening to 350 degrees. Toss pickles into egg wash then into bread crumbs. Shake off excess and carefully add to oil. Fry until golden brown, about 2 minutes. Remove and drain on a paper towel. Season with salt and pepper.

LOBSTER MAC 'N CHEESE

We didn't invent lobster mac 'n cheese, but we were smart enough to put it on the menu. Feel free to substitute claw or knuckle meat if you want to save the tails for something else. Crab is great in this too.

SERVES 6 – 8

CHEF TIP

Nothing feeds a hungry crowd around the holidays like this luscious hot mess. Take one bite and you'll be giving thanks, too. Good luck fighting grandma for seconds.

1 lb. box elbow macaroni, cooked

2 8-oz. lobster tails, cooked for 4 minutes and meat removed

1 oz. butter

8 sprigs fresh thyme

10 oz. white American cheese

2 cups heavy cream

3 oz. truffle oil

salt & pepper to taste

Preheat oven to 400 degrees. Chop lobster meat. Melt butter in saucepan. Add lobster and thyme and cook for 1 – 2 minutes. Add cheese, cream, truffle oil, salt and pepper to taste, stirring. Once melted, add macaroni and mix together. Turn into baking dish. Bake 20 minutes or until golden and crispy.

ONION RINGS

There are onion rings, and then there is a reason for living. We didn't realize we had stumbled on such a killer version until we tucked them in our Booty & Belly sandwich (page 156) and customers started asking for them as sides. They're easy and worth the effort, so there's no use in pretending otherwise.

SERVES 4

CHEF TIP
Serve with buttermilk tarragon dressing (page 176) or date ketchup (page 178). You won't hear any complaints.

- 1 quart vegetable oil or shortening
- 2 cups all-purpose flour
- 12 oz. of your favorite beer
- 1 tsp. sugar
- salt to taste
- 2 large Vidalia onions, sliced into ½" rings

Heat oil to 350 degrees. In a bowl, combine flour, beer, sugar, and salt. Stir until smooth. Dip each onion slice into batter and immediately lower into hot oil. Cook until golden, approximately 4 – 5 minutes. Place on paper towel to drain. Season with additional salt and serve while hot.

SOME SORT OF MAGIC
⋯❧ Lana Wright ❧⋯

Who she is: Co-owner of Senate; Dan's wife. **Her role:** She started out managing the front of the house. Now she's director of operations. Her job is to keep Dan in line, and the restaurants in order.

> **I'm from Cincinnati,** but I met Dan in Chicago. I'd bring him home to visit my family. He'd say, "I love it here. Let's move and start a restaurant." I thought it was so romantic. It meant I could have everyone I loved all in one place while pursuing my dream.

> **Dan was bartending because he refused** to take a chef job. That's just not how he wanted to introduce himself to Cincinnati. In hindsight, I see why he did it, but at the time I thought, "How are you not cooking? This is what you do."

> **When Dan decided on Over-the-Rhine** as the location for Senate, I was absolutely 100 percent against it. It was dangerous. It was a ghost of a neighborhood. But he saw something that I couldn't see because he didn't have a history with it. He could see the area was going to develop.

> **I never asked my immediate family for money.** I'd rather starve than ask. That's just how I am.

> **I said, "Let's have my uncle Diab** look at the space and if he says no, it's off." He was an experienced restaurateur, and I trusted him. I was convinced he'd side with me and say no. I couldn't believe he said yes.

> **I really thought I was going to serve** the whole dining room and Dan was going to cook. I thought I was going to be Flo, and he was going to be Mel from that old show *Alice*.

> **The day we opened there were people lining up outside.** There were fifteen people waiting, then thirty, and all of a sudden it was a clusterfuck. I was shocked. *Why are they here? What do they want? Are they here for this? Oh my God.*

> **A few weeks later,** I got out of bed and collapsed on the floor. We were working so hard—my legs just wouldn't stand. We started laughing and crying.

> **I felt as if I was in a fishbowl,** and everyone was watching. We were walking into the unknown, and it felt like we were going into war. In the restaurant business, if you don't come out swinging right away, you're done.

> **It was some sort of magic that happened.** How the menu was laid out, the simplicity of the design, the hot dogs—it was different than what anyone else was doing. I still feel like we're living in a dream.

"Suddenly everything that held me down couldn't hold me anymore. I couldn't justify being afraid."

FRIED CHEESE CURDS

**SERVES 5 – 6
APPETIZER PORTIONS**

CHEF TIP
I use fresh white cheddar curds from Blue Jacket Dairy in Bellefontaine, Ohio. If you can't find them at the store, you can order them online at bluejacketdairy.com

1 quart vegetable oil or shortening

2 eggs + ¼ cup water for egg wash

2 cups all-purpose flour

salt & pepper to taste

24 cheese curds

2 cups panko bread crumbs, run through food processor

In a 2-quart pot, heat oil or shortening to 350 degrees. In a bowl, combine flour, salt and pepper. Dip each curd into egg wash, then toss into seasoned flour. Dip in egg wash a second time, then bread crumbs. Carefully add to oil, fry until golden brown, about 2 – 3 minutes. Remove and drain on a paper towel-lined plate. Season with salt.

NOTES FROM A RETIRED LINE COOK
BY MARISSA GEIGER

I had just gotten out of a horrendous relationship and quit my job as a Montessori school teacher. I wanted to do something radical. I wanted to follow my heart. That's when I emailed Dan Wright and asked if he needed a hand in the kitchen. To my surprise, he said yes and hired me at the fry station. Every day I fried duck fat fries. I fried them until my legs and back surged with white-hot pain. I fried them until my mind tangled. I fried until I couldn't fry anymore. When I wanted to break down, Dan picked me up. "I see something in you," he'd say. "Keep pushing."

As time went by, those guys in the kitchen—including Dan—became my brothers. If anyone messed with me, they threatened to kill them. I remember looking at Yousef one day and saying, "I'm so happy I'm not sexually attracted to any of you," and both of us laughing. So for a year, that's how it was. I fried duck fat fries and exchanged raunchy jokes, and those guys made me feel like me again.

Eventually I wore out. I just did. The life of a line cook isn't for everyone, and ultimately it wasn't for me. But I will never forget those days. The heat. The fry oil. The friendship. Sometimes, you find yourself where you least expect it.

OYSTERS

SERVES 2 – 4

2 dozen fresh oysters
½ cup champagne mignonette (recipe follows)
½ cup hot sauce (recipe follows)
fresh lemons

CHEF TIPS

I prefer West Coast oysters like Fanny Bay, Naked Cowboy, Kusshi, and Kumamoto.

When shucking, fold a dish towel over your oyster knife and apply a solid amount of pressure. Make sure to keep your wrists well balanced on a cutting board. Angle the knife 90 degrees so you don't go through your hand.

CHAMPAGNE MIGNONETTE
YIELD: 1 CUP

5 oz. champagne vinegar
5 shallots, minced
3 oz. water
1 T. sugar
½ tsp. gingerroot, minced
cracked black pepper

Whisk ingredients together in a nonreactive bowl. Season generously with pepper.

HOT SAUCE
YIELD: 1 ½ CUPS

1 cup dried chiles
1 tsp. horseradish
1 tsp. cumin
1 cup white wine vinegar
1 garlic clove, minced
1 tsp. sugar
salt to taste

Soak chiles in water overnight, then remove seeds. Strain water. Place rehydrated chiles and remaining ingredients in blender and purée.

Shuck oysters. Serve with mignonette, hot sauce, and fresh lemons.

BONE MARROW

Bone marrow is easy to find at your local butcher. Though it's not common to see a heap of bones piled in the display case, there are usually some in the back. All you have to do is ask.

SERVES 4

1 cup olive oil

1 T. curry powder

1 T. ground cumin

salt to taste

2 lb. beef bones (16 medium), cut lengthwise into 3" pieces

shallot cranberry jam (recipe follows)

8 slices grilled bread (optional)

CHEF TIP
Don't have a band saw handy in the kitchen? Have your butcher cut the bones for you before you bring them home.

SHALLOT CRANBERRY JAM
YIELD: 2 CUPS

3 shallots, minced

1 T. olive oil

1 cup dried cranberries

1 cup pinot noir

1 tsp. Dijon mustard

2 T. sugar

salt & pepper to taste

Over medium heat in a small non-aluminum pan, sauté shallots in olive oil until caramelized. Lower heat, add rest of the ingredients and cook for about 15 minutes. Remove from heat and purée in blender. Refrigerate.

Preheat oven to 500 degrees. Combine olive oil with spices and rub mixture generously into each bone. Roast bones in an oven-safe dish for about 16 – 20 minutes. Season with salt. Serve with jam and grilled bread (optional).

UNDERDOGS

I mean come on, let's face it. You can't look very civilized eating a hot dog. No one ever has. Believe me, I would know. But that's why Senate works—it's not a place where you need to look any certain way. It's a place where you can relax and hang out while being served some really good fucking food. You can't take yourself too seriously when you're eating a hot dog called Natalie Porkman.

The name for Senate came a few years ago. I was sitting with Lana, and it suddenly dawned on me: dining out is all about coming together and sharing your points of view. The problem is that as many times as I explained the concept to potential investors, they either didn't get it or didn't get me.

I spent the first two years in Cincinnati running my business plan all over town, trying to get people interested. Until Kathleen Norris came along, things looked pretty grim. When I explained the concept to her, she just got it. Kathleen's job was to recruit businesses to Over-the-Rhine in an effort to revitalize the neighborhood. She put me in touch with 3CDC (Cincinnati Center City Development Corporation), who loaned us a generous amount of money for the build-out of the restaurant. Kathleen was not only a good person to have on my side, but just a hell of a good friend. I'll never forget the day I signed the lease. I was ecstatic, but I had to hold it in. Lana knew I wanted to sign, but because the spot was in a really rough neighborhood, she wasn't sure it was the right move. I waited for several months to tell her I had already signed the agreement, which turned out to be just enough time to get her warmed up to the idea. For the next sixteen months, we worked with an architectural firm to build the space and obsessed about every detail doing so: the bar, the materials, the fixtures. I called my dad—who had worked in the construction business—constantly to consult with him about one thing or another.

Once the build-out was done, the next battle started: raising enough money to buy the food, supplies, and equipment. Even though construction was complete,

This was the building before I signed the lease for Senate. Still a little rough around the edges.

the tables and chairs set up and ready to go, we couldn't open. My aunt had written a check for the first twenty-five thousand, but it wasn't enough to get the doors opened. We needed another forty grand, and we were stuck until then. No money. No food. No customers. Lana and I were fucking broke. I sold my car, and Lana sold all the Apple stock her father had left her. I was down to seven bucks in my bank account. We'd sit inside Senate—which was boarded up from the inside—and just hoped the money would come.

Miraculously, it did. Stephen Leeper, the president and CEO of 3CDC, introduced me to an angel investor who put up the rest of the cash. The deal was this: he'd fork over the dough, but if my business tanked, he'd take all the equipment and the liquor license and start over with someone else. I promised I wouldn't let him down and agreed to pay him back over the next four years.

It took half that time. Two years later, I invited him to lunch and slid a check across the table that covered the remainder of the balance. I also paid my aunt back the money she'd invested. Paying them was more important to me than paying myself. When it was finally done, I felt amazing. We were finally free.

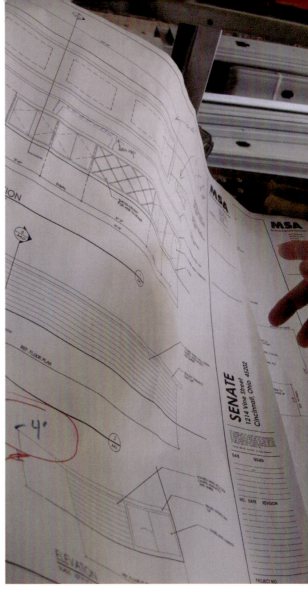

Kathleen Norris

Who she is: A consultant and realtor; principal of her own firm, Urban Fast Forward. **Her role:** Created the concept for the Gateway Quarter retail district in Over-the-Rhine and recruited the first phase of retailers and restaurants.

>**I got Senate done** because Dan promised me duck fat fries. I love duck fat. I'm the mother and daughter of chefs and consider duck fat one of the world's greatest foods.

>**3CDC is the master developer and investor** in Over-the-Rhine. My job was to persuade them that Dan and Lana—complete unknowns back then—were a good investment. They needed a lease and funding for the construction of Senate.

>**I kept saying, "Look at his credentials."** He had worked in L.A. He had cooked in Chicago for Chef Paul Kahan at Blackbird. Lana had unbelievably strong front-of-house skills. I thought they were a dream team.

>**The main trick was to keep getting meetings** so everyone could understand Dan's concept and see his passion. Restaurants are often a big risk for landlords.

>**I'm not unlike Dan** in that I'm just unbelievably stubborn in pursuit of what I believe is right.

>**Dan was relentless in pursuing 3CDC.** I remember writing an email to an executive over there. The subject line was, "Any Minute Now…" and the email read: "… Dan Wright is going to knock on my door. He's a very tenacious guy."

>**He looks at a trend, breaks it down,** and tries to figure out how to keep it pure while making it popular. He's a wonderful chef, but his greatest gift is that he's a restaurateur.

>**Dan isn't trendy.** He pays attention to what people are looking for, and he's able to get out in front of a movement. In any industry, that's what the really talented people can do.

>**He likes strong women.** In fact, he likes strong people. His team is super competent, and they stand up for themselves. The by-product is that Dan can run out of the restaurant for an hour or a day, and it runs exactly as if he were there. That's a gift.

>**In 2007, 12th and Vine** was the highest crime corner in Cincinnati. Seven years later, it's the hottest spot in town.

"You can tell pioneers because they're the ones with arrows in their chests. Dan and Lana were pioneers in Over-the-Rhine."

A closer look

HAUTE DOG

I spent my formative years in Chicago eating hot dogs like it was my job. It didn't matter the dive—Parky's, Gene & Jude's, Hot Doug's, Portillo's—I was there. Meanwhile, 300 miles away, my future wife was eating her fair share of them too. Before she was tall enough to see over the cash register, Lana was working at her father's Gold Star Chili, where cheese coneys were king. By the time we married, it would have been weird *not* to open a hot dog restaurant.

Still, we didn't want Senate to be the same old bag of tricks. We wanted it to stand out. That's when our special brand of gourmet dogs was born. Big knife-and-fork meals. Elevated in style, driven by fresh ingredients.

Sometimes they're inspired by a region or a dish—like the Hello Kitty Dog (page 77) with ponzu-wasabi slaw and wasabi mayonnaise, which tastes like a bite of Asia. Sometimes it's a celebrity in the news who greases our wheels—like the Honey Boo Boo (page 100) with sweet corn butternut relish and country fried bacon. This explains why I've got cooks—grown men—surfing *TMZ* and flipping through *OMG!* magazine. Looking for pop-culture inspiration is part of the job.

Dog Trick: Split the ends of your dogs with a knife in a crisscross pattern. That way they'll be perfectly cooked in the center with delicious crunchy bits on both sides.

In addition to seven fixture dogs on our menu, we feature a different dog-of-the-day five times a week (so far, there have been over 500). Most are easy enough to make at home without much trouble. Some are a little fussier and require a few days to prep. Mostly though, cooking our dogs is just about loosening up and having fun. If you've got a sense of humor, or if you're willing to try something new, you'll be just fine.

SUBSTITUTIONS

Don't sweat it if a recipe calls for a particular sausage like beef or pork, and you're not feeling it. Substitutes are fine. The following icons represent our recommendations for dogs that would be just as good as the original. Watch out for them in each recipe to truly make each dish your own.

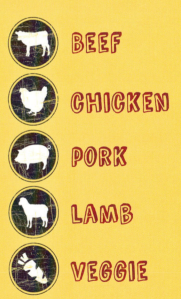

And another thing: we've got a whole section of recipes devoted to encased meat (page 172), so if you're one of those crazy ambitious cooks like us, make your own sausages and dogs, and earn full bragging rights.

TRAILER PARK

A fixture on the menu since Senate first opened, this dog is a lowbrow favorite—gritty, addictive, and insanely good. It's also the restaurant's best-selling dog, and one of the easiest to throw together when the whole family shows up for an afternoon of cornhole and beer.

SERVES 6

CHEF TIP

A Cincinnati icon for over 50 years, Grippo's BAR-B-Q potato chips have a spicy, sweet dust and vinegary wang that has developed a cult-like following even beyond the Ohio River Valley. Naturally, you can substitute your favorite barbecue chips or, better yet, get the Grippo's 1 1/2 lb. box mailed right to your door.

6 hot dog buns, buttered and toasted
6 all-beef hot dogs, grilled
6 slices American cheese
6 slices crisp bacon
3 cups coleslaw (page 190)
1 cup crushed Grippo's BAR-B-Q potato chips

Assemble in order:
bun + dog + cheese + bacon + slaw + grippo's

JIMMY THE GREEK

We went through a pretty intense gyro phase, making a weekly trek to Areti's Gyros in Findlay Market. Naturally, a dog followed. The key is the quality of the gyro meat, which is spun on a rotisserie and then sliced super thin.

SERVES 6

CHEF TIP
Everyone has their own version of tzatziki, but it all starts with great Greek yogurt or labneh.

- 6 hot dog buns, buttered and toasted
- 6 all-beef hot dogs, grilled
- 1 ½ cups lemony tzatziki (recipe follows)
- 12 slices or ¾ lb. gyro meat
- 6 slices ripe tomato, cut in half
- ½ cup red onion, shaved or thinly sliced
- ½ cup feta, crumbled

LEMONY TZATZIKI
YIELD: 2 ½ CUPS

- 1 medium English cucumber, seeded and diced into ¼" pieces
- 10 scallions, thinly sliced
- 2 cups plain Greek yogurt
- 3 sprigs of mint, leaves removed and chopped
- 3 sprigs of dill, leaves removed and chopped
- juice of 2 lemons
- 1 tsp. sugar
- salt & pepper

Mix all ingredients together in a bowl. Season to taste. Refrigerate until ready to use.

Assemble in order:
bun + dog + 1 tablespoon tzatziki sauce + gyro meat + remaining tzatziki + 2 tomato halves + shaved onion + feta

KOREAN

We've had this dog on our menu since opening day. Kimchi, a spicy, fermented cabbage, is the main event. We make our own white-boy version of it, which is a little less spicy and more pickled than fermented. Keep it easy and buy yours from a local Korean or Asian market.

SERVES 6

CHEF TIP

Braised beef short ribs (page 166) are an essential component in Senate cooking. Find them shredded on the Poutine Dog (page 92), Cabo (page 101), and Bollywood (page 117).

6 hot dog buns, buttered and toasted
6 all-beef hot dogs, grilled
½ cup harissa mayo (page 180)
1 ½ cups braised beef short ribs (page 166)
2 cups kimchi
1 cup quick pickled cukes (page 180)
1 T. sesame seeds, toasted

Assemble in order:

bun + dog + mayo + short ribs + kimchi + cukes + sesame seeds

SILENCE OF THE LAMB

We first served this dog at Senate to preview the flavors of our Mediterranean-inspired sibling restaurant, Abigail Street, which we opened next door in 2011. The fig relish is unbelievable as a topping, but it's pretty bangin' on its own, too. Make sure to use fresh figs at the peak of season.

SERVES 6

6 hot dog buns, buttered and toasted
6 merguez sausages (page 173), grilled
1 ½ cups baby arugula
6 oz. balsamic glaze (page 188)
½ cup crumbled goat cheese
2 cups Black Mission fig relish (recipe follows)

CHEF TIPS

Fig season generally lasts from June to September. Look for fruit that isn't too green, moldy, or wilted. The more shriveled figs appear, the longer they've been off the tree.

Pairs well with a nice Chianti!

BLACK MISSION FIG RELISH
YIELD: 2 CUPS

1 pint fresh Black Mission figs
½ cup red onion, finely diced
1 jalapeño pepper, seeded and minced
1 tsp. sugar
3 sprigs mint, leaves removed and chopped
3 sprigs cilantro, leaves removed and chopped
2 T. olive oil
salt to taste
juice of 2 limes

Remove stems from figs and slice into quarters. Mix with rest of ingredients, squeezing lime juice over last.

In a bowl, toss arugula with balsamic glaze.

Assemble in order:
bun + sausage + goat cheese + dressed arugula + fig relish

ONE NIGHT IN BANGKOK

Technically, we got this name from Murray Head whose song, "One Night in Bangkok," topped the charts back in the 80s. But the real story is that our juvenile kitchen humor got the best of us—we just liked hearing customers say "bang-kok" over and over. Aw c'mon, it's not like we're back in the kitchen quoting Whitman.

SERVES 6

6 hot dog buns, buttered and toasted
6 all-beef hot dogs, grilled
1 ½ cups spicy peanut sauce (recipe follows)
1 cup quick pickled cukes (page 180)
2 cups carrot & daikon slaw (page 191)
6 oz. Thai sweet chili sauce
½ cup fresh cilantro leaves
2 T. peanuts, toasted and chopped

CHEF TIP

Spicy peanut sauce is great in this recipe, but you can also make it sweeter by using brown sugar peanut sauce (page 185).

SPICY PEANUT SAUCE
YIELD: 1 ½ CUPS

3 T. chunky peanut butter
1 T. sriracha
¼ cup Thai sweet chili sauce
¼ cup mirin

Blend with whisk. Refrigerate.

Assemble in order:
bun + dog + peanut sauce + cukes + slaw + chili sauce + cilantro + peanuts

SLEEP WHEN WE DIE

The first six months at Senate were straight up brutal and terrible, and quite honestly I don't know how any of us survived. Lana and I knew it would be tough, but we figured our biggest challenge would be finding customers. We thought that in the beginning, it would be her serving, me cooking, and someone washing dishes.

That's not what happened. We opened at 11:00 on a Friday morning, and the place was slammed in fifteen minutes. I was scared shitless. I didn't know how we were going to make it. I had prepared the menu ahead of time and practiced the dishes with the cooks, but when the tickets started rolling in, everyone blanked. What could I do? I started handling every order myself, teaching everyone on the line like it was their first shift in a kitchen.

That was pretty much life at Senate for a long time. We were selling more food in our fifty-five-seat restaurant than I ever imagined: coming in every day and prepping from scratch, fighting our way through service, cleaning up, and doing it all over again. Working eighty-five hours a week under all that pressure took its toll on everyone. One of my line cooks went home, started cooking up some fries, and fell asleep with a pot of hot oil burning on the stove. When he woke up, his entire apartment was in flames. He had to jump from the fire escape to get out.

I look back now and see how hard we were pushing. One morning, Lana got out of bed and just collapsed on the floor. We immediately started laughing and crying. Every day felt like Groundhog Day.

There were good moments, too. Like any family, the tough times brought us closer together. Every night after service, when the last customer was gone, we'd hang around for hours together drinking and blowing off steam. Ultimately, not everyone was able to hang in there with us for the long haul, but some did, including Josh Treadway, who's now our general manager. I probably didn't deserve the endless solidarity he showed me during some of the hardest hours of our lives—but there he was, every day and every night, working his ass off, no questions asked.

Eventually, we learned to buy bigger containers, to prep a helluva lot more food, and to be more efficient about expediting and organization. Now, we can easily feed a roomful of people at any given time, but believe me when I say we've got battle scars. No matter how many more restaurants we open, nothing will ever be that hard. Nothing ever could be.

KITCHEN WISDOM WITH JEREMY MANIS

Jeremy, a chef at Senate, is part madman, part unicorn, part nutty professor. Taste one of his dogs, and you'll know. Since he's been working at the restaurant, he's helped create hundreds of feature dogs, each one weirder and more delicious than the last. Here are five things he knows about being successful in the kitchen (and in life).

1. **Be a sponge.** The more you know, the more you can teach. There's nothing like seeing your craft manifest itself in another person.

2. **Get all MacGyver on its ass.** The most versatile tool in the kitchen is a spoon. It's your vessel for tasting. Flip it over, and it's a spatula. Use two spoons, and you've got a pair of tongs.

3. **Don't be a pansy.** Don't just stick to what you know. Research. Look stuff up and learn. Get out of your comfort zone. Go for it, man.

4. **You can eat crap if it makes you happy.** Canned ravioli is okay if it reminds you of your childhood. Food should always have a sense of place and purpose.

5. **Be grateful.** Some of my favorite meals are simple and prepared by someone else. Making a meal for another human being is an act of hospitality, kindness, and service. Always say thank you.

JUST IN B BEAR

The pursuit of hedonism between two buns. Who doesn't love pretzels and barbecue sauce? It may be a little odd—maybe even a little over the top—but the girls go wild every time. And that's what's up.

SERVES 6

CHEF TIP

Feel free to substitute cream cheese for goat cheese here. Also, instead of crushed pretzels, try chopping up some soft pretzels.

6 hot dog buns, buttered and toasted
6 pork Vidalia sausages (page 172), grilled
6 slices crisp bacon
1 cup crumbled goat cheese
6 oz. Senate BBQ sauce (page 177)
1 cup caramelized onions (page 178)
½ cup crushed pretzels

Assemble in order:

bun + sausage + bacon + goat cheese + BBQ sauce + onions + pretzels

JESSE SPANO

When we were kids, *Saved by the Bell* was our babysitter until mom came home. Out of respect, we've featured dogs for most of the cast. Sure, Jessie may have been a little princess back in the day, but then we saw *Showgirls*. This dog is as memorable as that moment when we noticed Jesse Spano had grown up.

SERVES 6

CHEF TIP
If you want to do an A.C. Slater version, add 1 cup testosterone.

6 hot dog buns, buttered and toasted
6 all-beef hot dogs, grilled
6 slices sharp cheddar cheese
6 slices crisp black pepper bacon
1 ½ cups remoulade (page 190)
18 slices crispy fried pickles (page 31)

Assemble in order:
bun + dog + cheese + bacon + remoulade + fried pickles

MEXICO CITY

Our chef Jeremy might be a German-Irish white boy from Cincinnati, but when he bleeds, it's the colors of Mexico. This is one of his favorite dogs because it's south-of-the-border inspired—a great combination of guacamole and fried tortilla strips. Ahora puedes morir y ir al cielo.

SERVES 6

6 hot dog buns, buttered and toasted

6 all-beef hot dogs, grilled

6 slices crisp bacon

1 cup chipotle crema (page 187)

2 cups guacamole (page 176)

1 ½ cups crispy fried tortilla strips (page 186)

Assemble in order:
bun + dog + bacon + crema + guacamole + tortilla strips

JEREMY'S DEATHBEAD MEAL

He says his last supper will be stewed pork with salsa verde. We have to admit, it would be a killer way to go out.

SALSA VERDE, SERVES 6 – 8

1 white onion, chopped

½ bulb garlic, chopped

2 poblano peppers, roasted and skinned

6 tomatillos, roasted

juice of 1 ½ limes

handful of cilantro

½ cup water

salt to taste

Mix all in blender until slightly chunky. Transfer to a pot, bringing to a boil and simmering over low heat for 2 hours.

CROQUE MADAME

The croque-madame is a traditional grilled ham and cheese sandwich finished with a fried egg. Our hot dog version is one of my favorite dishes in the restaurant: gooey cheese, warm ham, béchamel, and a perfectly poached egg on top. Split the yolk open, take a bite, and go toward the light.

SERVES 6

6 hot dog buns, buttered and toasted
6 all-beef hot dogs, grilled
6 slices country ham, warmed
6 poached eggs
1 ½ cups béchamel, warmed
black pepper to taste

CHEF TIP

To poach the perfect egg, bring a pot of water to a rolling boil. Turn it down to medium, gently crack your egg in, and allow it to cook for 2 minutes, untouched. Pull it out with a slotted spoon and give it a little jiggle. If the egg white isn't set, drop it back in for 10 seconds.

BÉCHAMEL

YIELD: 2 CUPS

¼ lb. butter
¼ cup all-purpose flour
1 ½ cups heavy cream
4 oz. white American cheese, cubed
salt & pepper to taste

In a small pan, melt butter. Whisk in flour until smooth. Whisk in cream. Add cheese gradually and stir until thickened, about 3 – 4 minutes. Season to taste.

Assemble in order:
bun + dog + ham + egg + béchamel + pepper

GOING TO SEE A MAN ABOUT A DOG

Len Bleh, Avril-Bleh & Sons Meat Market

It's easy to get seduced by the one-stop mega-mart, that magical place where hot dogs and dish detergent live under one roof. Consider this a plea to visit your local butcher. He understands something your big box grocer doesn't. He knows—and actually cares about—what's going into your body. And that translates to better flavor.

Len Bleh is one such butcher. At his 120-year-old family-owned and operated business in downtown Cincinnati, meat comes from animals who have lived good lives in open fields. Hinds, quarters, and sides are processed fresh every day. To inject a sausage with filler or preservatives would be an unthinkable act of disrespect. Len is an honest man in a modest profession, an artist in a dying craft.

One day, just as he was finishing a fresh batch of sausage, I wandered in the shop. Len offered me a sample. "Here," he said. "Try this." It was simple and delicious, seasoned with salt, pepper, paprika, garlic, and just the slightest hint of cayenne. So good, in fact, I couldn't believe I had been getting my dogs from anywhere else.

I made quick plans to have Len create an original all-beef hot dog for Senate. Not only did it make sense to source locally, I desperately needed a purveyor who could keep up with our demands. Len was the guy. For six months, we worked together refining the recipe and adjusting the spice blend until it was perfect.

Today, Len grinds, stuffs, and smokes all our dogs exclusively and delivers them fresh every week. That's 4,000 dogs a month; 48,000 a year. And you know what? You can taste the love in every single one.

GOETTA SUPERSTAR

Think of this as a kickass breakfast dog. Goetta (pronounced get-uh), a mixture of ground pork, oats, and spices, tastes kind of like your morning sausage and oatmeal rolled into one. Don't skip the arugula here—it counteracts the salty meat with just the right amount of bitterness.

SERVES 6

CHEF TIP

In the 1800s, German immigrants added oats to ground pork to stretch rations over several meals. Since then, goetta has become a Cincinnati favorite showing up in everything from burgers to pizza.

6 hot dog buns, buttered and toasted
6 all-beef hot dogs, grilled
3 oz. butter
6 slices goetta (6" x 1" lengths) (page 173)
2 cups country gravy (page 184)
1 cup baby arugula
6 poached eggs
salt & pepper to taste

In a sauté pan, melt butter. Brown goetta on all 4 sides.

Assemble in order:
bun + dog + goetta + gravy + arugula + poached egg + salt & pepper

HELLO KITTY DOG

I couldn't think of a better way to commemorate my wife's fascination with Hello Kitty than with this Asian-inspired dog. Its combination of wasabi mayonnaise and carrot-cabbage slaw is sweet and spicy, just like her.

SERVES 6

6 hot dog buns, buttered and toasted
6 all-beef hot dogs, grilled
½ cup wasabi mayonnaise (page 177)
6 slices crisp bacon
3 cups ponzu-wasabi slaw (recipe follows)
¼ cup wasabi peas, crushed
1 T. sesame seeds, toasted

CHEF TIP

This wasabi mayonnaise is practically combustible. A little schmear will liven up any sandwich like the Booty & Belly (page 156). Or use it as a dip for the potstickers (page 122).

PONZU-WASABI SLAW
YIELD: 4 CUPS

2 cups cabbage, shredded
2 cups purple cabbage, shredded
1 cup carrots, shredded
1 cup wasabi mayonnaise (page 177)
¼ cup ponzu
1 T. black sesame seeds
1 T. white sesame seeds
salt to taste

Combine shredded cabbages and carrots in a bowl. Thoroughly mix in mayonnaise, ponzu, and sesame seeds. Season with salt. Refrigerate.

Assemble in order:
bun + dog + wasabi mayonnaise + bacon + ponzu slaw + crushed wasabi peas + sesame seeds

You get a dog!
You get a dog!
And you get a dog!

OKRA WINFREY

One evening, Farmer Sallie (page 137) delivered several pounds of okra harvested earlier in the day and bam!—there was the name for a daily dog. Okra has a long season, so this makes for a great cold-weather dog when partnered with spicy andouille sausage and remoulade. Make your remoulade as hot as you like by adding or subtracting sugar and sriracha to taste.

SERVES 6

6 hot dog buns, buttered and toasted
6 andouille sausages (page 172), grilled
6 slices crisp bacon
1 cup remoulade (page 190)
2 cups crispy fried okra (recipe follows)

CHEF TIP

Don't hate on okra. If it's fresh, it's not going to be slimy. In fact, fresh okra tastes so sweet and flavorful, you can even slice it and eat it raw.

CRISPY FRIED OKRA

1 quart vegetable oil or shortening
2 cups finely ground cornmeal
1 cup all-purpose flour
1 tsp. smoked Spanish paprika
1 lb. fresh okra, stems removed and sliced
2 medium eggs + ¼ cup milk for egg wash
salt to taste

In a 2-quart pot, heat oil or shortening to 350 degrees. In a bowl, mix cornmeal, flour, and paprika. Toss sliced okra in egg wash, then in cornmeal mixture. Carefully add okra to hot oil. Fry until golden brown, about 2 minutes. Remove and place on a paper towel-lined plate. Season with salt.

Assemble in order:
bun + sausage + bacon + remoulade + okra

LINDSEY LOWHAN

We're just gonna call it like it we see it—pure mayhem in a bun. You can't eat this dog without getting messy. The goat cheese melts and oozes. The balsamic is sticky to the touch. And yeah, it's addictive enough to send you into rehab.

SERVES 6

CHEF TIP
This dog is also great topped with crispy fried onions (page 187).

- 6 hot dog buns, buttered and toasted
- 6 all-beef hot dogs, grilled
- 1 cup goat cheese, crumbled
- 2 cups baby arugula
- ¾ cup caramelized onions (page 178)
- 6 oz. balsamic glaze (page 188)
- 6 slices crisp bacon

In a bowl, mix half of the goat cheese with arugula, caramelized onions, and 4 ounces of the balsamic glaze. (The remaining crumbled goat cheese and balsamic glaze are used in the assembly.)

Assemble in order:
bun + dog + crumbled goat cheese + bacon + arugula mixture + balsamic glaze drizzle

LINDSEY LOWHAN (PAGE 82)   TRAILER PARK (PAGE 55)   HELLO KITTY DOG (PAGE 77)

BOSS HOG

Named after our favorite villainous glutton from *The Dukes of Hazzard*, this dog features pork belly, beer, and fried pickles. It's like we died and went to heaven Rosco.

SERVES 6

CHEF TIP
Pairs well with a white cowboy hat and cigar.

6 hot dog buns, buttered and toasted

6 all-beef hot dogs, grilled

2 cups BBQ pork belly (page 169), heated

1 ½ cups Kentucky Bourbon Barrel Ale cheese (page 185)

18 slices crispy fried pickles (page 31)

Assemble in order:
bun + dog + BBQ pork belly + beer cheese + pickles

UNA NOCHE CON NICK LACHEY

We put this dog on our menu so that Nick Lachey could be available to the ladies every night. It's since become our most tweeted dog—with a surprising amount of scandalous content.

SERVES 6

STAR STUD
Crazy but true: when Nick comes into the restaurant, the guys in the kitchen are actually more excited than the girls in the dining room.

6 hot dog buns, buttered and toasted
6 all-beef hot dogs, grilled
1 cup chipotle crema (page 187)
2 cups roasted mushroom & poblano salsa (page 189)
1 ½ avocados, sliced thin
2 T. fresh cilantro leaves
¼ cup queso fresco, crumbled
18 – 24 slices pickled jalapeños (page 179)

Assemble in order:
bun + dog + crema + salsa + avocado + cilantro + queso + pickled jalapeños

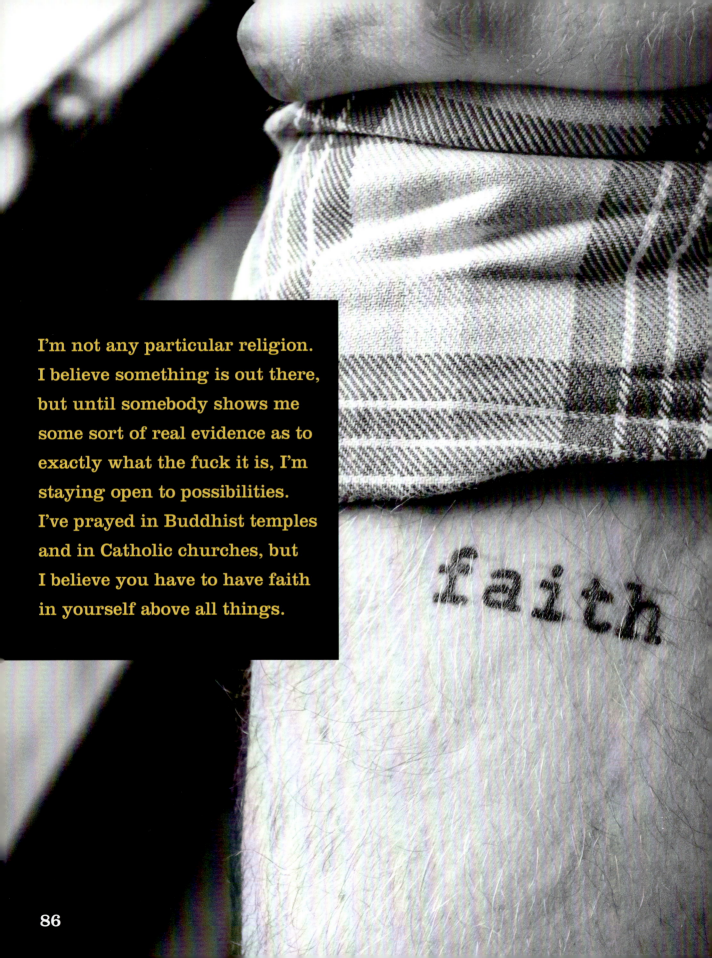

I'm not any particular religion. I believe something is out there, but until somebody shows me some sort of real evidence as to exactly what the fuck it is, I'm staying open to possibilities. I've prayed in Buddhist temples and in Catholic churches, but I believe you have to have faith in yourself above all things.

CUBAN

Everybody in our kitchen loves a good Cuban sandwich. Pork, mustard, pickles, cheese, and rye bread? Come on, now. We use a banana Dijon for a tropical island twist. With the brown sugar pork sausage, it's a perfect balance of sweet and savory.

SERVES 6

CHEF TIP
Bananas are surprisingly versatile. You can use them instead of flour in nearly anything. Bread, pancakes, you name it.

6 hot dog buns, buttered and toasted
6 brown sugar pork sausages (page 172), grilled
6 slices Swiss cheese
6 slices country ham, warmed
6 oz. roasted banana Dijon (page 191)
1 ½ cups braised pork belly (page 168), warmed
24 slices homemade pickles (page 27)

Assemble in order:
bun + sausage + cheese + ham + Dijon + pork belly + pickles

89

WHITE TRASH WEDDING

Two of my favorite things together: beer cheese and bacon. Best if consumed in an old recliner with *Duck Dynasty* on the television. Also the perfect appetizer to a cigarette and another six pack.

SERVES 6

WATCH THIS WHILE EATING

My Name Is Earl
Cops
Eastbound & Down
Pawn Stars
Joe Dirt
Anything Jeff Foxworthy

6 hot dog buns, buttered and toasted
6 all-beef hot dogs, grilled
6 slices crisp bacon
1 ½ cups beer cheese (page 185)
6 oz. Senate BBQ sauce (page 177)
3 cups coleslaw (page 190)
1 ½ cups crispy fried onions (page 187)

Assemble in order:
bun + dog + bacon + beer cheese + BBQ sauce + slaw + fried onions

POUTINE DOG

Poutine is our most popular dish at Senate, so creating this dog was a no-brainer. It's an insane combination of truffle fries, short ribs, and cheese curds. The result can be summarized in three words: instant crowd-pleaser.

SERVES 6

CHEF TIP
Want to bring your A-game to dinner? Have your cheese curds shipped from Wisconsin for the real deal.

6 hot dog buns, buttered and toasted
6 all-beef hot dogs, grilled
¾ cup cheese curds
1 cup poutine gravy (page 184)
3 dozen truffle fries (page 24), 6 fries per dog
1 ½ cups braised beef short ribs (page 166)
6 poached eggs
salt & pepper to taste
2 T. fresh thyme, chopped

In a saucepan over low heat, stir cheese curds and poutine gravy together.

Assemble in order:
bun + dog + fries + curd / gravy + short ribs + egg + salt & pepper + thyme

MADAME CLEO

She ran a psychic line for six years and was an alleged shaman—so maybe she saw this voodoo magic coming. A spicy, jerk chicken dog with all the island flavors you'd expect from a wiener named after her likeness. Only one downside to making this dog: the first three minutes don't come free.

SERVES 6

CHEF TIP
Save leftover buttermilk dressing for another day. It's great on our grilled peach salad (page 128).

6 hot dog buns, buttered and toasted

6 jerk chicken sausages (page 173), grilled

8 oz. buttermilk tarragon dressing (page 176)

3 cups grilled vegetable relish (recipe follows)

GRILLED VEGETABLE RELISH
YIELD: 3 – 4 CUPS

1 zucchini, cut in half lengthwise

1 yellow squash, cut in half lengthwise

1 red onion, sliced into 4 thick slices

2 T. olive oil

4 sprigs mint, leaves torn

salt & pepper to taste

Prepare grill to medium heat. Rub vegetables with 1 tablespoon olive oil. Grill until tender. Cool then chop. Mix with remaining olive oil, mint leaves, salt and pepper.

Assemble in order:
bun + sausage + dressing + grilled vegetable relish

BRAT MICHAELS

Just like Poison—our favorite glam metal band from the 80s—this dog is loud, unapologetic, and nothing but a good time. Shreddin' with caramelized onions, and driven by the power ballad of apple bacon relish, your job is just to open up and say… Ahh!

SERVES 6

6 hot dog buns, buttered and toasted
6 bratwursts (page 173), grilled
1 cup brown sugar Dijon (recipe follows)
1 cup caramelized onions (page 178)
2 cups apple bacon relish (recipe follows)

FAVORITE BRET MOMENTS

"Every Rose Has Its Thorn"

Rock of Love, seasons 1-3

The official Roses & Thorns fragrance

Celebrity Apprentice 3

BROWN SUGAR DIJON

YIELD: 1 ¼ CUPS

1 cup spicy Dijon mustard
2 T. dark brown sugar
1 T. honey

In a small mixing bowl, stir together Dijon, brown sugar, and honey. Refrigerate.

APPLE BACON RELISH
YIELD: 3 CUPS

1 lb. thick-cut applewood smoked bacon, cut into ½" pieces

1 medium yellow onion, diced

4 Granny Smith apples, peeled, cored, and chopped into ½" dice

3 T. butter

½ cup dark brown sugar

salt to taste

Place bacon in a medium skillet and cook over low heat. Add onion and apples; sauté until caramelized. Add butter and brown sugar; stir until sugar dissolves. Season with salt.

Assemble in order:
bun + bratwurst + Dijon + onions + relish

SARAH JESSICA PORKER

She may be known for bringing sex to the city, but we love her because she's from the 'burbs of Cincinnati. This dog is a little sophisticated, a little quirky, and a lot like Carrie Bradshaw minus the closet space.

SERVES 6

6 hot dog buns, buttered and toasted
6 pork Vidalia sausages (page 172), grilled
6 oz. red pepper aioli (recipe follows)
2 cups sweet corn country relish (recipe follows)
6 poached eggs
salt & pepper to taste

CHEF TIP

Try basil mayo (page 180) as a topping here, using cilantro instead of basil.

SWEET CORN COUNTRY RELISH

YIELD: 3 CUPS

3 ears sweet corn
1 medium red onion, chopped
1 oz. olive oil
½ lb. country ham, small dice
12 stems cilantro, leaves removed and chopped
3 T. apple cider vinegar
1 tsp. sugar
salt to taste

Remove kernels from cob. Sauté onion in olive oil. Add corn and ham and cook 3 minutes. Remove from heat. In a bowl, mix ham, onion, and corn together with cilantro, vinegar, sugar, and salt.

RED PEPPER AIOLI

YIELD: 2 CUPS

3 red bell peppers
1 oz. olive oil
1 cup mayonnaise
1 T. garlic, minced
1 tsp. sriracha

Preheat oven to 500 degrees. Toss peppers in olive oil. Place on sheet pan and roast until skin blisters. Place in bowl and cover in plastic wrap for 30 minutes or until skin is easy to peel off. Rinse under cool water to remove skin and seeds. Purée with rest of ingredients. Refrigerate.

Assemble in order:
bun + sausage + aioli + relish + egg + salt & pepper

HONEY BOO BOO

SERVES 6

6 hot dog buns, buttered and toasted
6 all-beef hot dogs, grilled
1 ½ cups honey Dijon (page 189)
6 slices country fried bacon (page 28)
2 cups sweet corn butternut relish (recipe follows)

CHEF TIP
Goes well with a 2-liter of Mountain Dew. Nothing like 248 grams of sugar to keep you fresh-faced for the crowd.

SWEET CORN BUTTERNUT RELISH
YIELD: 2 CUPS

1 small butternut squash
3 T. extra virgin olive oil
2 ears of sweet corn, kernels removed
1 small red onion, chopped
3 sprigs of thyme, leaves removed
1 sprig of basil, leaves removed and chopped
1 tsp. honey
1 tsp. Dijon mustard
salt and pepper to taste

Peel butternut squash, cut in half, and remove seeds. Dice squash into ¼" pieces. In sauté pan, warm 1 tablespoon olive oil over medium heat. Add squash and cook, stirring occasionally. Once the squash is slightly soft, add the corn and chopped onion. Continue to sauté for 5 minutes. Remove from heat and place in a mixing bowl. Refrigerate for 20 minutes. When squash mixture has cooled, stir in chopped herbs, honey, remaining olive oil, and Dijon. Season with salt and pepper.

Assemble in order:
bun + dog + Dijon + bacon + more Dijon + relish

CABO

SERVES 6

6 hot dog buns, buttered and toasted

6 all-beef hot dogs, grilled

6 oz. chipotle crema (page 187)

1 cup braised beef short ribs (page 166)

2 cups guacamole (page 176)

1 ¼ cups queso fresco, crumbled

1 ½ cups crispy fried tortilla strips (page 186)

Assemble in order:
bun + dog + crema + short ribs + guacamole + queso fresco + tortilla strips

It's Brittany
(page 104)

IT'S BRITTANY

Oops!... we did it again. This dog loves being the center of attention, but she's not for everyone. If you're going to embrace her, you've got to enjoy foie gras—buttery, rich, and everything your mother warned you about. Who knows? This dog just might be your gateway to fandom.

SERVES 6

CHEF TIP
Peach preserves add a twist of Southern femme fatale.

6 hot dog buns, buttered and toasted
6 pork Vidalia sausages (page 172), grilled
2 cups red leaf lettuce, torn
6 oz. balsamic glaze (page 188)
1 cup peach preserves (page 138)
12 slices foie gras torchon (page 140)
salt & pepper to taste

In a bowl, toss lettuce with half of the balsamic glaze. Reserve remainder for drizzling atop assembled dog.

Assemble in order:
bun + sausage + dressed lettuce + preserves + 2 slices torchon + balsamic glaze + salt & pepper

THE ELVIS

We recommend that you do not consult your doctor before eating this hound dog and have a soft pillow nearby for when you're finished. The combination of peanut butter, banana, and bacon is so love-me-tender delish that you'll wake up crying in the chapel.

SERVES 6

MY TOP FIVE ELVIS SONGS
"Burning Love"
"Viva Las Vegas"
"Suspicious Minds"
"That's Alright Mama"
"A Little Less Conversation"

6 hot dog buns, buttered and toasted
6 brown sugar pork sausages (page 172), grilled
3 oz. peanut butter
3 oz. roasted banana Dijon (page 191)
6 slices crisp bacon
¼ cup honey
6 slices foie gras torchon (page 140)
2 bananas, sliced
salt & pepper to taste

Assemble in order:
bun + sausage + peanut butter + Dijon + bacon + honey + torchon + bananas + salt & pepper

NATALIE PORKMAN

I can't promise eating the Natalie Porkman will transform you into the perfect combination of physical beauty and intellectual fortitude. But I can guarantee beer cheese. And that's something.

SERVES 6

CHEF TIP
Pepper bacon is cured in a wet brine of salt, sugar, and spices for several days. It's then smoked and rolled in cracked black peppercorns to finish.

6 hot dog buns, buttered and toasted
6 bratwursts (page 173), grilled
6 slices crisp black pepper bacon
2 cups chipotle beer cheese (page 185)
2 cups crispy fried onions (page 187)

Assemble in order:
bun + bratwurst + bacon + beer cheese + fried onions

Top 5 celebrities my wife wishes we would name a hot dog after:
1. Ryan Gosling 2. Ryan Gosling
3. Ryan Gosling 4. Ryan Gosling
5. Ryan Gosling

JERSEY SHORE

SERVES 6

6 hot dog buns, buttered and toasted
6 pork fennel sausages (page 172), grilled
¼ cup torn basil leaves
2 cups tomato, eggplant & onion relish (recipe follows)
1 cup fresh mozzarella, chopped

CHEF TIP
This vegetable relish rocks on any kind of pork or chicken sausage.

TOMATO, EGGPLANT & ONION RELISH
YIELD: 3 CUPS

1 ½ cups cherry tomatoes
1 small eggplant, large dice
1 medium red onion, chopped
1 red bell pepper, chopped
1 T. minced garlic
½ cup olive oil
¼ cup red wine vinegar
1 T. sugar
salt & pepper to taste
4 stems fresh basil, leaves removed and chopped

Preheat oven to 400 degrees. Combine all ingredients except for basil. Roast for 25 minutes or until caramelized. Remove from oven and mix in basil.

In a bowl, mix together basil leaves, relish, and mozzarella.

Assemble in order:
bun + sausage + basil, relish and mozzarella mixture

PRINCE HARRY

His brother gets to be king, so we thought we'd give the poor bastard a dog in our book. You're welcome.

SERVES 6

FAVORITE GINGERS

Molly Ringwald
Jessica Rabbit
Lucille Ball
Elmo
Opie
Ginger Spice
Axl Rose
Willie Nelson
Daphne from *Scooby Doo*
Mario Batali

6 hot dog buns, buttered and toasted
6 pork fennel sausages (page 172), grilled
6 slices crisp bacon
1 ½ cups refried black beans (page 186)
1 ½ cups roasted poblano beer cheese (page 185)
1 ½ cups crispy chorizo (page 172), crumbled
¼ cup cilantro leaves

Assemble in order:
bun + sausage + bacon + beans + beer cheese + chorizo + cilantro

FAMILY MATTERS

There are three things you need to be able to do as a chef and restaurant owner: cook, manage numbers, and keep your shit together when you're managing people. When we started Senate, I had the first two down. It took time for me to develop the third. Don't get me wrong, sometimes yelling can be a fruitful motivator, but I've learned that for most people, it only takes a whisper.

Lana and I both realize that job security is really important. We want people to know that if they work hard, they'll always have a job with us. Even if someone fucks something up, it doesn't usually benefit me to let them go. I have time and money invested in their potential. It's a lot more effective for me to help them turn a bad situation around.

Granted, I expect a lot from everyone who works with me, but I'm also willing to do a lot in exchange—whether that means writing someone a check if they're down and out, giving them an extra meal, or inviting them to our house for the holidays. If any of our staff needs a place to celebrate, our home is open. We don't want anyone to feel like they're not a big part of what we're doing.

Every year, I take a handful of staff to another city—like New York or Chicago—for the weekend. Lana and I cover the expenses. In return, we ask that everyone stay hungry and not get too drunk. It's an important ritual for us, because it builds camaraderie and exposes us to food and hospitality trends in other cities. We get to see what other chefs are up to, what kind of food they're making, how their service stacks up. My job as a business owner is to bring out the best in my people—so that's what I get up every morning and try to do.

Senate Vocabulary

THE GAMECHANGER

The period between 10:00 and 10:30 when the kitchen staff is free to crack open a couple of beers. After all, they've already worked for twelve hours and have served 300 people. You may still be hanging out in the dining room noshing on duck fat fries, but these guys are dog-tired and ready for a drink.

THE ATTITUDE ADJUSTMENT

On Fridays and Saturdays, just before closing time, the bartenders are free to have a drink or two. Most of the customers are already gone, and if they're not, they're trickling out. Senate is almost closed for business, and it's time to shift gears.

JOSH

Josh is like my little brother. I met him at Twist in Cincinnati, where he was a barback. When I told him about my idea for Senate, he quit almost immediately and started to help me make it happen. He had never eaten one thing I cooked, but he had my back. At Senate, he's moved from bartender to bar manager to general manager. I can honestly say he's one of the most dedicated people I've ever met.

RODRIGO

Rodrigo is one of the best cooks we have. He's got insane skills. No one works the grill better, and no one works faster. He actually reminds me of this guy Miguel who used to beat my ass when I was a line cook in Chicago. Oh, and one more thing: don't ever call Rodrigo a Mexican. He's from Guatemala, and the last thing you want to do is call a Guatemalan a Mexican. You can get killed for that.

ILYAS

Ilyas worked with Lana and me in Chicago at Souk, and he's the only person at Senate who knew both of us individually before we dated. When we opened the restaurant, we asked him to move here and manage the front of the house. He packed his car and drove it straight to the restaurant. He crashed on our couch until he got a place of his own, and in the meantime, towed the line at Senate. In 2011, when we opened Abigail Street, our second restaurant, he became the general manager. He's one of the brightest and most reliable people we know.

JEREMY

Jeremy joined the team early on, and he's an absolute workhorse. He cooks three or four days a week, and he expedites the remaining two or three. The thing about Jeremy is that he just gets it. He gets our philosophy. Actually, out of anybody I work with, he's the guy who knows what I'm going to say before I say it. That means a lot in this business.

MIKE

Before we hired him as a bartender at Senate, Mike and I worked together at Twist in Cincinnati and nearly duked it out a couple of times. He thought I was the worst bartender in the world and had terrible customer service skills. He still does. But I've got to hand it to the guy, the customers love him. He's also an incredibly innovative guy with creative, off-the-wall ideas—like aging rum in bourbon barrels years before it became cool. Mike respects the craft and loves what he does. And what the hell, I love Mike.

NACHO MAN RANDY SAVAGE

Cowboy hat. Cape. Glitter. Sunglasses. It only works if you're Randy Savage. In many ways, his wrestling fame was eclipsed by his wacky appearances in Slim Jim commercials. No better inspiration for this dog, which is just as bold and audacious. Ohhh, yeeeeahh!

SERVES 6

6 hot dog buns, buttered and toasted
6 all-beef hot dogs, grilled
2 cups chorizo refried beans (page 186)
1 ½ cups Slim Jim beer cheese (page 185)
1 cup pico de gallo (recipe follows)
1 cup crushed Fritos
18 – 24 pickled jalapeños (page 179)

CHEF TIP

There are a variety of Slim Jim flavors, from Tabasco to chipotle to Jamaican jerk. This is your excuse to play around and try them all.

PICO DE GALLO
YIELD: 3 CUPS

1 jalapeño pepper, seeded and chopped
2 medium ripe tomatoes, finely chopped
1 medium red onion, finely chopped
3 T. olive oil
1 garlic clove, minced
1 bunch cilantro, leaves removed and chopped
2 T. white wine vinegar
1 tsp. sugar
juice of 2 limes
salt to taste

Combine all ingredients in a bowl. Season to taste. Refrigerate until ready to use.

Assemble in order:
bun + dog + refried beans + beer cheese + pico de gallo + Fritos + pickled jalapeños

BOLLYWOOD

This is all Bollywood, baby. A little flashy, a little confusing, entirely delicious. Braise the curried short ribs for something to do while you're watching one of the epic, three-hour-long films. Mango chutney is strongly recommended. Singing and dancing are optional.

SERVES 6

6 hot dog buns, buttered and toasted
6 all-beef hot dogs, grilled
1 cup cilantro yogurt (page 188)
1 ½ cups curried beef short ribs (page 167)
1 ½ cups mango chutney (recipe follows)
¼ cup fresh cilantro leaves

CHEF TIP

Don't focus on color when choosing mangoes at the market. The best indicator for freshness is if they give a little under the pressure of your thumb.

MANGO CHUTNEY
YIELD: 4 CUPS

4 ripe mangoes, peeled and diced
1 large red onion, chopped
juice of 3 limes
1 bunch cilantro, leaves chopped
1 jalapeño pepper, seeded and chopped
½ cup dried cranberries
½ cup raisins
¼ tsp. curry powder
1 T. olive oil
1 T. white wine vinegar
salt to taste

Combine all ingredients in a bowl. Season with salt to taste. Allow to stand for one hour until ready to use.

Assemble in order:
bun + dog + yogurt + short ribs + chutney + cilantro

CAPTAIN JENKINS

Before the birth of our twins, Knox and Oliver, our two Yorkshire terriers were the babies in the house. This dog is named after them, Milo and Lulu Jenkins, who also ran around the restaurant off-hours. For a while, the guys in the kitchen would feed them sausage scraps. No wonder their favorite chew toy is a fake plastic hot dog.

SERVES 6

6 hot dog buns, buttered and toasted

6 all-beef hot dogs, grilled

6 slices crisp bacon

6 oz. charred scallion miso aioli (recipe follows)

18 pieces fried cheese curds (page 38)

3 oz. Thai sweet chili sauce

CHEF TIP
Fried cheese curds (page 38) are also amazing on their own as a small bite or appetizer.

CHARRED SCALLION MISO AIOLI
YIELD: 1 ½ CUPS

6 scallions, ends trimmed

1 cup mayonnaise

1 T. brown miso paste

1 T. olive oil

1 T. water

salt to taste

Preheat grill to high. Grill scallions for 2 – 3 minutes until wilted and slightly charred. Chop lightly. Purée with rest of ingredients in blender. Refrigerate.

Assemble in order:
bun + dog + bacon + miso aioli + cheese curds + chili sauce

& SAVORY

POTSTICKERS

Boom. These just happened. Part potstickers, part crab rangoons. Crunchy, salty, pork wontons served with cream cheese. Believe me when I say they're freakin' awesome.

SERVES 4

CHEF TIP
The key to this dish is the balance of flavors. The sweet chili sauce is crucial to mellow out the salty pork.

1 quart vegetable oil or shortening

24 wonton wrappers

1 ½ lb. ginger pork sausage (page 172)

2 eggs + ¼ cup water for egg wash

salt & pepper to taste

1 cup Thai sweet chili sauce

1 cup miso cream cheese (recipe follows)

1 T. sesame seeds, toasted

½ cup scallions, chopped

MISO CREAM CHEESE

3 T. brown miso paste

8 oz. cream cheese, room temperature

1 T. lukewarm water

Whisk all together in a bowl. Refrigerate.

In a 2-quart pot, heat oil to 350 degrees. On a cutting board, lay out 12 wonton wrappers. Place 1 tablespoon of sausage in the middle of each. Brush egg wash around the edges. Fold into triangle, sealing the edges, and pushing out the air. Drop into the hot oil and cook for 4 – 5 minutes until crispy. Repeat with remaining 12. Drain on paper towels, season with salt and pepper. Serve with sweet chili sauce and miso cream cheese. Garnish with sesame seeds and chopped scallions.

PIG TAILS

If you like ribs, you'll love pig tails. They're a cheaper cut of pork, but with a very similar flavor. If you don't see them in the display case up front, ask your local butcher if he's got any in the back, or have him order them for you. Make sure to cut off the excess fat when you're cleaning the pig tails to get the right texture.

**SERVES 6 – 8
APPETIZER PORTIONS**

CHEF TIP

The outside of your pig tails should be crispy but not too crunchy. Make sure your pot of frying oil is up to temperature before frying them.

5 lb. pig tails
3 T. gingerroot, peeled and chopped
juice and rind of 2 oranges
1 quart vegetable oil or shortening
1 ½ cups all-purpose flour
2 cups Senate BBQ sauce (page 177)
1 bunch scallions, chopped
¼ cup cilantro leaves, torn
¼ cup sesame seeds, toasted

Use the same braising method for the pig tails as for the pork belly (page 168), adding gingerroot, orange juice, and rind to the braising liquid. Cool 2 hours. When pig tails are cool to touch, trim excess fat. In a pot, heat oil to 350 degrees. Dredge each pig tail in flour and fry in oil until crispy. Toss in BBQ sauce, sprinkle with chopped scallions, cilantro, and sesame seeds.

Josh Treadway

Who he is: General Manager of Senate.
His role: Oversees the dining room, expedites, crunches daily financials, manages staff, coordinates building maintenance, and pretty much anything else that might make your brain explode.

>**When I first met Dan,** we were both bartending. I thought he was abrasive. Now I think he's one of the best people in my life.

>**When he told me** about his hot dog concept, I'll be honest—I had my doubts. But I believed in Dan and believed if anyone could make it happen, he could.

>**I quit my job immediately and spent** the next few months helping Dan and Lana get the restaurant ready.

>**Lana showed me by example** how a restaurant should be managed. I've learned so much from her. Eventually, she gave me the keys and let me drive.

>**Our meetings in the office** can be a lot of fun, but they can also be intense because Dan and Lana are both incredibly direct. If we make a mistake, the office transforms into a war room.

>**He threatened to fire me** at least three or four times in the first week or two we were open. I think he felt the pressure.

>**That's just how brothers are**. Dan painted a future for me when I had nothing. When we started, he said we'd be in national magazines. Since then, we've been in *Forbes* magazine, *Rachel Ray*, and *Food & Wine*. Dan has a way of making you believe him.

>**I didn't have much of a future** before Senate. Dan took me under his wing and changed my life.

>**I get off work at one in the morning** and fall asleep at two or three. It's hard to have a personal life. I speak for anyone in this industry when I say it's tough.

>**A chef can make the most amazing dish,** but if the service staff is rude or indifferent, you'll lose customers.

>**We've never spent money on advertising.** We've been blessed with word-of-mouth and good reviews. Like anything worth achieving, success is a reflection of hustle and passion, good people, and hard work.

"I believe the front door is the most important part of a restaurant. The hello and goodbye are critical."

GRILLED PEACH SALAD

SERVES 4

CHEF TIP
Use peaches when they're at the peak of flavor in the summer. You can substitute nectarines or any stone fruit in season.

2 ripe peaches, halved and pit removed
1 T. olive oil
6 cups of your favorite greens, hand torn
8 slices of applewood smoked bacon, chopped and cooked crisp
6 oz. buttermilk tarragon dressing (page 176)
8 oz. goat cheese, crumbled
salt & pepper to taste

Toss peach halves in olive oil. Place on hot grill cut-side down. Grill 2 minutes on each side. Remove from heat. Chop. Add chopped peaches to lettuce along with crispy bacon and dressing. Divide among plates. Sprinkle with crumbled goat cheese. Season with salt and pepper.

POUTINE

On Senate's opening day, the first order was for poutine. Lana took one look at the dish and said, "I'm not serving this!" She thought it looked completely disgusting. Yeah, it's sort of an ugly duckling—but it's comforting and absolutely delicious. I love the way the cheese curds are about the same size as the fries—so when you're taking a bite, you're never really sure which you're going to get. I don't remember how I convinced Lana that our diners would love it, but I did. It has since become the superstar of our menu.

POUTINE

Poutine is a French-Canadian dish I first tasted on a trip to Montreal. This is my somewhat refined spin on it. Instead of the traditional brown gravy and cold cheese curds, I like to warm the curds up in chicken gravy and top it with short ribs.

SERVES 4 – 8 DEPENDING ON YOUR WILL TO LIVE

CHEF TIP

You can make one giant tray of this and serve it at a party, or you can divide it among 8 plates and serve individual appetizer portions.

3 cups poutine gravy (page 184)

2 cups cheese curds

1 recipe truffle fries (page 24)

2 cups braised beef short ribs, braising juice included (page 166)

2 T. fresh thyme

4 poached eggs (optional)

salt & pepper to taste

Warm gravy over low heat. Crumble curds into gravy; heat for an additional minute. Divide fries among 4 plates. Cover with gravy and curds. Top with ½ cup short ribs per plate. Sprinkle with fresh thyme leaves. Optional: Top with poached egg and season with salt and pepper.

MY WIFE'S SALAD

Because we're pretty meat-centric at Senate, it was important to Lana to balance our menu with some greens. This is a salad she makes for me at home. It's great on its own, but I can't resist topping it with grilled meat—steak, chicken, fish, or whatever we've got handy when dinner rolls around.

SERVES 4

8 cups baby arugula

⅓ cup balsamic vinaigrette (recipe follows)

3 T. shallots, minced

1 ½ cups cherry or grape tomatoes, cut in half

1 ½ cups buffalo mozzarella, cubed

salt & pepper to taste

1 avocado, peeled and sliced thinly

CHEF TIP

This salad will only be as good as the ingredients that make it. We get our tomatoes and arugula from Sallie Ransohoff (page 137), whose Sallie & Son's Farm outside of Cincinnati sets the standard for freshness.

BALSAMIC VINAIGRETTE

YIELD: 2 CUPS

1 cup balsamic vinegar

2 T. Dijon mustard

1 T. sugar

salt to taste

¾ cup extra virgin olive oil

Combine first four ingredients in blender. Slowly add olive oil to emulsify. Adjust seasoning to taste.

In a mixing bowl, toss all ingredients except avocado. Season with salt and pepper. Divide among 4 salad plates and top with avocado slices.

FARMER SALLIE

Sallie & Son's Farm

Sallie is the real deal. She rolls up at Senate's back door on Tuesday and Friday nights around 10:30 with crates and crates of beautiful fresh produce: herbs, tomatoes, mustard greens, potatoes, okra—you name it. Every spring she asks if there's anything I'd like her to grow, so I give her a short list.

There are not many farmers who will do that. Sallie is a great person—goofy and easy to get along with—and you can taste the love in everything she grows. She's exactly the kind of farmer I'm proud to support.

PBJ & F

SERVES 4

1 cup of your favorite peanut butter
8 slices white sandwich bread
8 slices foie gras torchon (page 140)
1 ½ cups cherry preserves (recipe follows)
4 T. butter
salt to taste
1 cup balsamic glaze (page 188)

CHEF TIP

For peach preserves, remove the pits from 3 peaches and roast in a 350-degree oven for 20 minutes. Chop, and follow the rest of the recipe.

CHERRY PRESERVES
YIELD: 3 ½ CUPS

2 cups Bing cherries, pitted
1 ⅔ cups sugar
3 T. lemon juice
1 ½ T. pectin

In a saucepan over low heat, combine fruit, sugar, and lemon. Add pectin and bring to a boil. Remove from heat. Refrigerate.

Divide peanut butter among 4 slices of bread. Place 2 slices of torchon on top of peanut butter. On remaining 4 slices of bread, spread the cherry preserves.
In a nonstick sauté pan, melt 1 tablespoon of butter. Place sandwich in pan and immediately flip it over so that it soaks up remaining butter. Fry on both sides until golden brown. Repeat with remaining sandwiches. Sprinkle with salt. Cut in half or quarters and serve with balsamic glaze.

SWEET POTATO FALAFEL

SERVES 4

2 cups dried chickpeas
1 large yellow onion, finely chopped
3 cloves of garlic, minced
½ cup flat-leaf Italian parsley, chopped
¼ cup cilantro, chopped
1 T. ground cumin, toasted
2 teaspoons baking powder
¼ teaspoon cayenne pepper
salt to taste
1 small sweet potato, peeled, roasted, and mashed
1 quart vegetable oil
1 cup cilantro yogurt (page 188)

Place dried chickpeas in a bowl, cover with cold water, and soak overnight. Drain chickpeas and combine with onion, garlic, parsley, cilantro, toasted cumin, baking powder, cayenne pepper, and a pinch of salt. Force the mixture through a meat grinder. Once ground, thoroughly stir in the sweet potato purée. The result should be a thick paste.

Form the mixture into balls approximately the size of a golf ball. Flatten slightly for more even cooking. In a large pot, heat the oil to 350 degrees. Fry falafel until golden brown, about 5 – 7 minutes. Remove and place on a paper towel to drain. Season with salt. Serve with cilantro yogurt for dipping, or wrapped in Lebanese flatbread with the yogurt, lettuce, chopped tomatoes, hummus, and pickles.

CHEF TIP

Since the chickpeas are not cooked (they cook once they hit the hot oil), a meat grinder is essential for creating the proper texture. No grinder? No worries. Try this alternate method (although we're not as fond of the softer texture): Mash or purée 2 cups of cooked or canned chickpeas. Mix with ingredients and follow instructions per recipe.

FOIE GRAS TORCHON

Making a torchon is a multistep project, so start it a day or two in advance. It lasts in the fridge covered in salt for several weeks, which makes it easy to come up with something on the fly. At Senate, we slice it on a couple of our dogs: It's Brittany (page 104) and the Elvis (page 105). It's also the star of our PBJ&F (page 138), but there's a huge wow factor when it's simply served with toast points and cherry preserves (page 138).

SERVES 24

CHEF TIPS

Pink curing salt is great for preserving meats like salami or goose liver.

For something special, freeze your torchon and then shave it with a microplane on top of poutine (page 133), fries (page 24), eggs, or even pasta.

2 lb. (1 lobe) foie gras, room temperature
3 cups milk
2 T. sugar
salt & pepper to taste
¼ cup brandy
3 T. pink curing salt

Spread lobe of foie gras open and remove cluster of arteries. Place in a glass baking dish and pour milk over it. Refrigerate overnight. Next day, remove foie gras from milk and pat dry. Flatten with hands, season with sugar, salt and pepper and pour brandy over. Let sit at room temperature for 30 minutes.

Transfer to cheesecloth. Roll up jellyroll-style into a log and tie ends with twine. Bring a 3-quart pan of water to a near boil. Drop the cheesecloth-wrapped foie into water for 2 minutes, then submerge into ice water for 5 minutes. Re-roll into tight log; re-tie both ends. Chill for a minimum of 2 hours. Store in the refrigerator covered with the pink curing salt for several weeks.

MC SCHNITZEL

Of all the pork sandwiches we've created, this is one of my favorites. It's a twist on the classic German schnitzel, a fried meat patty made from veal, pork, or chicken. Here, the pork is shredded and mixed with Dijon mustard for something a little different.

SERVES 4

CHEF TIP

You can substitute the garlic thyme aioli in this recipe with honey Dijon (page 189).

2 lb. braised pork belly (page 168), shredded
1 T. Dijon mustard
¾ cup all-purpose flour
2 eggs + ¼ cup water for egg wash
1 ½ cups panko bread crumbs, run through food processor
2 T. olive oil
1 oz. butter
3 sprigs thyme
4 brioche or egg buns, buttered and toasted
4 T. garlic thyme aioli (page 181)
4 lettuce leaves, bibb or red leaf, torn
½ cup apple bacon relish (page 95)

Add Dijon to shredded pork and form into 4 – 5 oz. patties, ½" thick. Dip into flour; shake off excess. Dip in egg wash, then bread crumbs. Panfry in olive oil over medium heat for 3 – 4 minutes. Flip and cook other side for 2 minutes. Add butter and thyme sprigs to pan; baste patties.

To assemble sandwich:
bun + garlic thyme aioli + lettuce + warm, crisp Schnitzel + apple bacon relish

GREEN CORN TAMALE

This is a cool twist on a classic tamale. Instead of using dried cornhusks, we use fresh ones. They impart a sweeter flavor and have an earthy, summery smell when you cut them open.

SERVES 12

CHEF TIP

Masa harina is made from field corn that is dried, cooked with limewater (which lends it a distinct flavor), then ground and dried.

8 ears of corn; remove husks and reserve
2 ½ cups masa harina
1 ½ cups cold water
1 ½ cups lard or rendered pork fat
1 cup chipotle crema (page 187)
2 cups roasted mushroom & poblano salsa (page 189)
1 ½ cups braised pork belly (page 168), shredded (optional)

Remove kernels from cob. Purée 1 cup of kernels. Mix the remaining kernels with puréed corn, masa, cold water, and lard. Tear strips of 1 or 2 husks into thin ribbons to use as ties. Set aside.

Lay two green husks crosswise. Place ⅓ cup of the masa mixture in the center. Fold into a package. Tie with strips. Repeat with remaining husks. Steam in a colander over a pot of boiling water for 5 – 7 minutes. Remove; cut open and top with a generous tablespoon each of chipotle crema, mushroom & poblano salsa, and shredded pork belly (optional).

BACON AND EGG SALAD

SERVES 4

CHEF TIP
My favorite combination of lettuces for this salad is frisée and red leaf.

6 cups of your favorite lettuce, hand torn
1 T. olive oil
8 slices bacon, chopped
12 fingerling potatoes, roasted and sliced into rounds
6 oz. tarragon vinaigrette (recipe follows)
4 eggs, poached
salt & pepper to taste

TARRAGON VINAIGRETTE
YIELD: 1 ½ CUPS

10 sprigs fresh tarragon, leaves removed
1 medium shallot, minced
½ cup champagne vinegar
1 T. sugar
salt & pepper to taste
¾ cup extra virgin olive oil

Combine first five ingredients in blender. Slowly add olive oil to emulsify. Adjust seasoning.

Place lettuce into a mixing bowl. Heat olive oil in a sauté pan and cook bacon until nearly crisp. Add potato slices and brown for an additional 1 – 2 minutes. Remove from heat. Add vinaigrette to pan. Pour over lettuce. Toss and divide among 4 salad plates. Top with a poached egg. Season with salt and pepper.

MUSSELS CHARMOULA

When we first opened, we had a beer-braised mussel dish on the menu, but it wasn't selling that well. Lana insisted that I switch it out for this recipe, which I used to make at Souk in Chicago. It's still her very favorite mussel dish in the world. The secret is the charmoula sauce—a blend of spices and fresh tomatoes. Customers will eat the mussels and drink the sauce straight from the bowl. We easily go through 100 pounds of mussels a week.

MUSSELS CHARMOULA

SERVES 4

2 T. shallots, minced
1 T. olive oil
1 lb. mussels (approximately 30 – 40)
2 cups charmoula sauce (recipe follows)
3 T. butter
1 tsp. sriracha sauce
8 sprigs cilantro, leaves removed

CHEF TIP

This recipe makes a lot of sauce. Have plenty of grilled bread for dipping.

CHARMOULA SAUCE
YIELD: 1 GALLON

1 large yellow onion, chopped
15 garlic cloves, chopped
2 oz. olive oil
12 Roma tomatoes, chopped
1 tsp. saffron, soaked in ice water
3 oz. sriracha sauce
15 sprigs cilantro, leaves removed and chopped
1 lb. butter
3 cups chicken stock (substitute with vegetable or seafood if desired)
1 quart heavy cream
salt & pepper to taste

Sauté onions and garlic in olive oil. Once they begin to caramelize, add tomatoes, saffron, sriracha, cilantro, and butter. Cook for 5 minutes, stirring. Reduce heat to low. Add stock and cream. Simmer for 1 hour until reduced by half, stirring occasionally. Remove from heat and cool to room temperature. Add salt and pepper. Purée in blender.

In a pot over high heat, sauté shallots in olive oil for 1 minute. Add mussels; stir for 1 minute. Cover with sauce. Add butter and sriracha. Cover and continue to cook on high for 5 minutes more. Adjust seasoning. Place in serving bowl, top with cilantro, and serve with lots of grilled bread.

SCALLOPS, LEEKS & SALSIFY

SERVES 4

6 pieces salsify, peeled and sliced in ¼" rings

8 oz. butter

1 large leek, sliced in half lengthwise, cleaned and sliced crosswise

2 cups heavy cream

salt & pepper to taste

¼ cup rendered bacon, chopped (optional)

16 medium or 12 large scallops

1 T. olive oil

1 oz. butter

In saucepan over medium heat, sauté salsify in 2 ounces butter about 3 minutes. Add leeks; cook 3 minutes more. Reduce to low heat; add cream and remaining 6 ounces of butter, stirring occasionally for 15 minutes or until it has the consistency of risotto. Season to taste with salt and pepper. Add bacon if desired. Keep warm while preparing scallops.

Season each scallop with salt and pepper. Heat olive oil over high heat in large nonstick skillet. Place each scallop seasoned side down in hot oil. Sear 2 minutes. Turn 90 degrees. Allow to cook 1 minute more. Flip over. Add 1 ounce butter to pan, basting top of scallops. Cook 1 minute. Remove from pan.

To assemble:
Place generous amount of warm leeks and salsify in bowl with wide rim. Arrange 3 large or 4 medium scallops atop. Great accompanied with roasted carrots or parsnips.

CHEF TIPS

Salsify is a long, thin root similar to a parsnip but with an oyster-like flavor and usually available in late summer to early winter.

Only pepper one side of the delicate shellfish so as not to overpower the flavor.

TURNING TABLES
BY ILYAS BOURCHID

When dining out, evaluating the food and service is part of the deal. Your experience matters to us, so the service staff is observing you, too. In four years of managing both Senate and its sister restaurant Abigail Street, here are a few things I've learned about you.

1. **You crave community.** The closer the tables, the more fun you're having. At Senate, you're sharing elbow room, which means you're relaxing, talking to people, and forming new relationships. This is why we love our job.

2. **You like a man with confidence.** If you don't like a dish I've recommended, I'll buy it for you. Straight up—that's how much I believe in Dan's food. I've never done that at any other restaurant.

3. **It's the little things that count.** I may not remember your name, but I try to remember something about you—what you like to eat, where you like to sit, or what sports team you follow. This matters. I can see it on your face.

4. **You might still be talking about me in 50 years.** I'll never forget the time I served churros at Table 100, only to discover the young couple getting engaged. I returned with a bottle of champagne and took a bunch of photos to help them remember the night.

5. **Blowing off steam is good for all of us.** After the restaurant closes for the evening, we turn off the lights and change the music. Anything goes: alt-country, ghetto hip-hop, 80s new wave. Taking the time to relax makes us better for you the next day.

LAMB BURGER

We frequently serve this at our sibling restaurant Abigail Street. It is the lyrical truth. Eat one and see the face of God.

SERVES 4

CHEF TIP
Combining lamb with a little beef counteracts some of its gaminess, adding fat and richness.

- 1 lb. ground lamb
- 8 oz. ground beef
- 1 small red onion, chopped fine
- ¼ cup flat-leaf parsley, chopped fine
- 3 garlic cloves, minced
- 1 T. baharat seasoning
- salt & pepper to taste
- 4 brioche or egg buns, buttered and toasted
- 4 lettuce leaves
- 1 cup goat cheese, crumbled
- 1 cup caramelized onions (page 178)
- 6 oz. date ketchup (page 178)

Heat grill to high. In a large bowl, combine meats, onion, parsley, garlic, and seasonings; mix well by hand. Form into 4 meatballs. Line a plate with wax paper and gently press each meatball to flatten to ¾" thick. Grill to medium, or desired temperature. Remove from grill and assemble.

To assemble sandwich:
bun + lettuce + lamb burger + goat cheese + caramelized onions + date ketchup

BOOTY & BELLY

We used to have a version of this sandwich called the Jennifer Lopez, made with pork butt and pork belly. Hell to the yes. We eventually changed the recipe and the name to suit, but the idea is the same: Pork. Slaw. Onion rings. Mind blown.

SERVES 4

4 brioche or egg buns, buttered and toasted

1 ½ cups BBQ pork belly (page 169), shredded and heated

1 cup celery root apple slaw (recipe follows)

8 onion rings (page 35)

½ cup Senate BBQ sauce (page 177)

8 slices homemade pickles (page 27)

CHEF TIP

Use a 2:1 ration of meat to slaw on the sandwich, so that when you squish it down, it oozes into a beautiful mess.

APPLE CELERY ROOT SLAW

YIELD: 2 CUPS

1 medium celery root, peeled

2 Granny Smith apples, peeled

1 small red onion, peeled

½ cup mayonnaise

1 tsp. celery seed

1 oz. rice wine vinegar

6 sprigs cilantro, leaves removed and chopped

Slice celery root, apples, and onions, then julienne. Combine all ingredients together and season to taste.

Assemble sandwich:
bun + BBQ pork belly + celery apple slaw + onion rings + sauce + pickles + love

LOBSTER BLT

I always know when a customer has ordered the lobster BLT, because I can smell the browned butter perfuming the entire restaurant. It kills me every time. There is just nothing sexier than a lobster tail with browned butter on a toasted bun.

SERVES 4

CHEF TIP
Get ready. Your house is about to smell just like Senate.

2 8-oz. lobster tails
3 T. butter
1 T. fresh thyme, chopped
salt to taste
4 brioche or egg buns, buttered and toasted
4 pieces bibb or red leaf lettuce
4 thick slices ripe tomato
8 slices crisp bacon, each cut in half crosswise
¼ cup basil mayo (page 180)

In a large pot, bring water to boil. Drop in lobster tails and boil exactly 4 minutes. Remove immediately and drop in a bowl of ice water to arrest cooking. With kitchen shears, cut each tail in half lengthwise. Remove meat and cut down the middle lengthwise again without cutting all the way through. Meat should be rare. Open it up and lay flat (butterflying) to widen.

In a large sauté pan over medium heat, melt 2 tablespoons butter. Add thyme and salt to taste. Add lobster meat and brown for 2 minutes. Flip over and add remaining tablespoon of butter, basting tails. Cook for another minute. Season with a pinch of salt. Remove. Reserve browned butter from pan for sandwich.

Assemble sandwich:
bun + lettuce + tomato + lobster + drizzle of browned butter + 4 half slices bacon + generous spoonful basil mayo

SENATE BURGER

Why have a dozen different burgers on the menu when this one is so supremely badass—it's the only burger we need to represent. Use a combination of ground meats for the most flavor.

SERVES 6

CHEF TIP
Go the extra mile here and make your own pickles (page 27).

1 lb. short ribs, cubed
1 lb. chuck, cubed
1 ½ lb. sirloin, cubed
1 T. Dijon mustard
salt & pepper to taste
6 slices cheddar
1 ½ cups caramelized onions (page 178)
6 brioche or egg buns, buttered and toasted
6 leaves bibb or red leaf lettuce
6 slices garden ripe tomato
18 slices homemade pickles (page 27)
6 oz. harissa mayo (page 180)

Mix short ribs, chuck, sirloin, Dijon, salt and pepper in a bowl. Push through meat grinder. Form into 6 large meatball-sized patties. Place patties on the grill over indirect heat (not directly over flame). Cook 2 minutes, turn 90 degrees. Cook 2 minutes more. Flip. Cook 2 minutes more, turn 90 degrees. Add cheese and onions and cook for an additional 2 minutes.

To assemble sandwich:
bun + lettuce + tomato + burger + pickles + harissa mayo

STREET FIGHT

The 12th and Vine Street intersection was more dangerous when we first opened, which is why Lana is the real badass in this story. I was back in the kitchen making mussels a hundred times a day while she was in the front by the door, dealing with the neighborhood head-on.

People would wander in every day asking for money. Or worse, they'd stand by the cash machine installed ten feet from our door, and beg customers on their way in. Asking for money so close to an ATM is illegal, so I'm not exaggerating when I tell you Lana has called the police dozens of times.

One day, a guy tried to apply for a job without a shirt on. "Let's proceed in this order," she said. "You put on a shirt, and I'll give you an application." We had to laugh. I'm not sure that kind of thing happens a lot in the suburbs.

The worst incident happened about six months after we opened. It was 6:00 in the evening when Lana went out the back door to have a smoke. As she took a couple of drags, she watched this kid wind his way down Jackson Street, getting closer and closer to where she was standing. When he was about two feet away, he suddenly pulled out a gun and pointed it at her. "Give me your money," he demanded.

She still talks about how he moved the gun up and down slowly, pointing it at her face, then her legs, then again at her face. She didn't have any money on her, so she just begged him not to do anything stupid. For whatever reason, he didn't. Something spooked him, and he quickly ran off, leaving her standing there scared to the bone.

It was a difficult situation, because we couldn't tell anyone other than the police what happened. Since people were already skeptical of the neighborhood, we couldn't risk scaring customers or losing our business. After that, the police really stepped up their game in the neighborhood. They went from patrolling once a day to every hour. The way we saw it, if this was a street fight, we were going to win or go down trying.

Now we look around at all the new businesses that have trickled in over the last few years, and the hundreds of people who line the streets on a daily basis shopping and dining, and it's a completely different vibe. I give a lot of credit to 3CDC, who's been managing the redevelopment of Over-the-Rhine for the last ten years and investing in businesses like ours. It couldn't have happened without them or the hard-core supporters who believed in the neighborhood's potential from the start. It also wouldn't have happened without people like us—crazy and just stupid enough to risk it all for a dream.

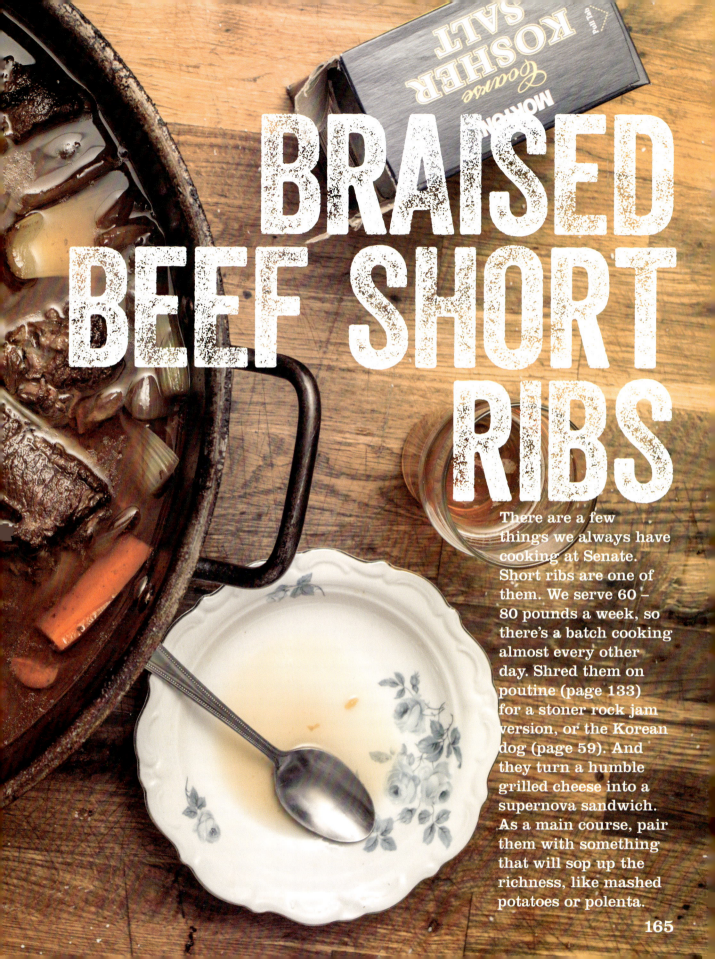

BRAISED BEEF SHORT RIBS

There are a few things we always have cooking at Senate. Short ribs are one of them. We serve 60 – 80 pounds a week, so there's a batch cooking almost every other day. Shred them on poutine (page 133) for a stoner rock jam version, or the Korean dog (page 59). And they turn a humble grilled cheese into a supernova sandwich. As a main course, pair them with something that will sop up the richness, like mashed potatoes or polenta.

BRAISED BEEF SHORT RIBS

SERVES 10

5 lb. beef short ribs
salt & pepper to taste
½ cup olive oil
2 cups red wine
2 medium carrots, peeled and chopped
2 small yellow onions, peeled and chopped
1 bunch celery, chopped
8 garlic cloves, chopped
2 quarts demi-glace (page 182)
2 T. sriracha sauce
10 sprigs thyme
2 bay leaves

Preheat oven to 450 degrees. Season short ribs with salt and pepper. In a large sauté pan, heat 2 tablespoons of olive oil. Once the oil is hot, place short ribs in pan and sear each side until browned. Remove from pan and set aside. Repeat until all short ribs have been seared. Deglaze the pan by pouring the red wine into the hot skillet and scraping off the caramelized bits.

In a large roasting pan, heat remaining olive oil. Add chopped carrots, onion, celery, and garlic and sauté until caramelized. Add the short ribs, covering with demi-glace and deglazed pan juices. Add sriracha, sprigs of thyme, bay leaves, and a generous pinch of salt and pepper.

Cover the roasting pan with aluminum foil and place in oven for 3 hours. Remove foil and cook uncovered 30 minutes longer. This will allow the short ribs to caramelize and the braising liquid to reduce. Remove the short ribs from the roasting pan and strain the braising liquid through a fine-mesh sieve. Place both the short ribs and the braising liquid in the refrigerator until ready to use or serve the short ribs warm and discard bones.

CHEF TIP

Curried beef short ribs are a kicked-up take on the standard. We serve them on our Bollywood dog (page 117).

VARIATION

CURRIED BEEF SHORT RIBS

3 T. olive oil
1 small yellow onion, finely chopped
1 T. madras curry

Heat olive oil over medium heat in a small sauté pan. Add onions, sautéing until caramelized. Add curry and stir. Add this mixture to short ribs after braising.

BRAISED PORK BELLY

We use a lot of pork products at Senate, and this is one of our favorites. Like the braised beef short ribs, I recommend serving this dish with something to soak up its juices—polenta, root vegetables, or potatoes.

SERVES 10

CHEF TIP
Great shredded on the Booty & Belly (page 156) and the Mc Schnitzel (page 141).

5 lb. pork belly
½ cup olive oil
1 can of your favorite beer
2 medium carrots, peeled and chopped
2 large yellow onions, peeled and chopped
1 bunch celery, chopped
20 garlic cloves, chopped
2 quarts chicken stock
2 T. Szechuan peppercorns
10 sprigs thyme
2 bay leaves
salt & pepper to taste

Preheat oven to 400 degrees. Slice pork belly into 6" pieces. Heat 3 tablespoons of olive oil in a large sauté pan over medium high heat. When olive oil begins to smoke, carefully place one piece of pork belly into the pan. Sear until golden. Flip and sear other side until golden. Remove pork belly and repeat as many times as necessary. Set aside. Carefully add one can of your favorite beer to the hot pan and stir to deglaze.

In a large roasting pan, heat remaining olive oil. Add carrots, onions, celery, and garlic. Sauté until vegetables are caramelized. Add pork belly, cover with chicken stock and pan juices to cover. Add peppercorns, sprigs of thyme, bay leaves, and two generous pinches of salt. Cover the pork belly with aluminum foil and braise for 3 hours. After 3 hours, remove aluminum foil and cook uncovered for an additional 30 minutes. This will allow the pork belly to gain a beautiful color and for the braising liquid to reduce.

Once the pork belly is finished cooking, remove from oven and allow to cool in braising liquid for 30 minutes to increase tenderness. Remove from the roasting pan and strain the braising liquid. Place pork belly and braising liquid into separate containers and refrigerate until ready to use. Pork belly can be sliced or shredded.

VARIATION

BBQ PORK BELLY

Shred braised pork belly. Add pork with 2 cups of braising liquid and 2 cups of Senate BBQ sauce (page 177) to a saucepan over medium-low heat. Simmer until hot.

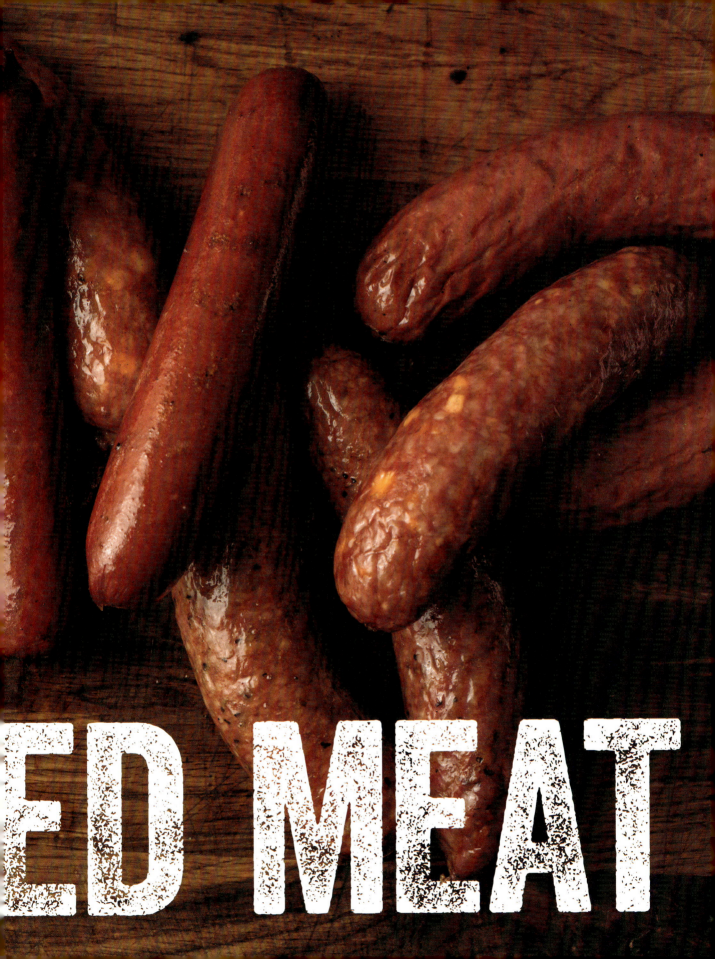

YIELD: 12 6" LINKS

ENCASED MEAT

Casing Method (for all recipes except where noted): Purchase 8' of hog casing from your butcher. Attach one end over sink faucet; run cool water through to rinse sodium out. Remove. Secure one end over tube of grinder. Push meat through. Place on a flat surface. Squeeze out excess air and tie off ends. Measure off 6" lengths. Gently crimp and twist each section. With a sterilized needle, poke a few holes into each link. This will prevent them from splitting when you grill them. Store in the refrigerator until ready to use.

PORK VIDALIA

2 lb. pork shoulder
½ lb. pork fat
1 medium Vidalia onion, chopped
2 T. garlic, minced
1 tsp. thyme, chopped
½ tsp. cumin
salt & pepper to taste

Before stuffing the casing to make links, cook up a small amount of sausage in pan to taste, then adjust seasoning where necessary.

BROWN SUGAR PORK

2 lb. pork shoulder
½ lb. pork fat
1 small onion, chopped
2 T. brown sugar
1 tsp. dried sage
1 T. maple syrup
salt to taste

This doubles as a good breakfast sausage for patties.

GINGER PORK

2 lb. pork shoulder
½ lb. pork fat
1 medium onion, chopped
1 T. garlic, minced
1 T. gingerroot, minced
1 tsp. lime zest
1 tsp. orange zest
¼ cup cilantro, chopped
1 tsp. ponzu
salt to taste

If you can't find ponzu, substitute 1 teaspoon soy sauce and the juice of 1 lime.

PORK FENNEL

2 lb. pork shoulder
½ lb. pork fat
1 medium onion, chopped
2 T. garlic, minced
1 red bell pepper, chopped
3 T. fennel seeds, toasted and crushed in a mortar & pestle
1 tsp. smoked paprika
½ tsp. cayenne
salt to taste

ANDOUILLE

2 lb. pork shoulder
½ lb. pork fat
1 medium Vidalia onion, chopped
2 T. garlic, minced
½ tsp. cayenne
½ tsp. file powder
½ tsp. cumin
1 tsp. smoked paprika
½ lb. Tasso or country ham, chopped into small dice
salt & pepper to taste

Grind all except Tasso, then mix in.

CHORIZO

2 lb. pork shoulder
½ lb. pork fat
1 medium Vidalia onion, chopped
2 T. garlic, minced
2 T. smoked paprika
¼ cup sherry vinegar
1 tsp. cumin
salt & pepper to taste

PORK APPLE FENNEL

2 lb. pork shoulder

½ lb. pork fat

1 medium onion, chopped

1 T. garlic, minced

2 Granny Smith apples, peeled and diced

1 fennel bulb, chopped, sautéed in olive oil, and cooled

- -

BRATWURST

2 lb. pork shoulder

½ lb. pork fat

½ lb. veal

1 small onion, chopped

1 tsp. white pepper

1 tsp. cumin

1 tsp. nutmeg

salt to taste

Put through grinder 3x for a superfine texture.

MERGUEZ

1 ½ lb. lamb shoulder, cut into small dice

1 ½ lb. chuck roll, cut into small dice

1 medium onion, chopped

2 T. garlic, minced

1 tsp. red pepper flakes

1 tsp. smoked paprika

1 tsp. cumin

½ tsp. ground coriander

½ tsp. cinnamon

salt & pepper to taste

For a great breakfast, place some of the ground sausage in a baking dish, cover in your favorite tomato sauce flavored with 1 teaspoon ground fennel seed and a generous amount of black pepper. Crack a few eggs over and bake in a 400-degree oven for 20 minutes.

- -

JERK CHICKEN SAUSAGE

1 lb. chicken breast, chopped

2 lb. boneless chicken thighs, skin on and chopped

1 medium yellow onion, chopped

3 T. garlic, minced

2 T. jerk seasoning

salt to taste

GOETTA

YIELD: 10 – 12 SERVINGS

2 ½ lb. pork shoulder

½ lb. pork fat

2 cups steel-cut oats, cooked in 1 quart water or chicken stock, and drained

1 large onion, chopped

½ tsp. cumin

½ tsp. smoked paprika

salt & generous amount pepper

Mix all ingredients and push through grinder. Place in a wide pot and cook for 20 – 25 minutes or until browned. Press into oblong baking dish. Chill 2 hours. Cut into 6" x 1" rectangles.

PANTRY

BUTTERMILK TARRAGON DRESSING

YIELD: 2 CUPS

CHEF TIP
Think of this as ranch dressing with a little more love. Insanely good on a BLT, and works great on a wedge salad or anything with bacon.

20 sprigs fresh tarragon, leaves removed
1 ½ cups buttermilk
1 cup mayonnaise
salt & pepper to taste

Purée tarragon, buttermilk, and mayonnaise in a blender. Season generously with salt and pepper.

GUACAMOLE

YIELD: 4 CUPS

8 ripe avocados, peeled, pitted, and chopped
1 jalapeño pepper or Serrano chili, seeded and chopped
juice of 4 fresh limes
1 large red onion, chopped
1 medium heirloom tomato, chopped
2 garlic cloves, minced
1 bunch cilantro, leaves removed and chopped

Mash avocados in bowl. Stir in chopped chili and lime juice. Add onion, tomato, garlic, and cilantro. Season with salt.

SENATE BBQ SAUCE

YIELD: 1 QUART

CHEF TIP
Kentucky Bourbon Barrel Ale rocks in this recipe, but even cheap beer will do.

2 oz. olive oil
1 medium yellow onion
4 garlic cloves, minced
½ can chipotles in adobo sauce, peppers peeled and seeded
2 cups ketchup
1 cup brown sugar
1 tsp. cumin
16 oz. beer
salt to taste

In a pot over medium heat, sauté onions and garlic in olive oil. Add remaining ingredients. Slowly simmer for about an hour. Remove from heat; cool. Purée in blender until smooth. Refrigerate.

WASABI MAYONNAISE

YIELD: 2 CUPS

2 cups mayonnaise
1 T. powdered wasabi or 2 T. freshly grated wasabi
½ cup water
juice of 1 lime
salt to taste

Purée ingredients in blender. Season to taste. Refrigerate.

CARAMELIZED ONIONS

YIELD: 3 CUPS

3 red onions, sliced

2 T. olive oil

½ cup water

pinch of salt

Sauté onions in olive oil over high heat for about 4 minutes. As the onions begin to caramelize, add the water and a pinch of salt. Reduce heat to medium and continue to cook, stirring, for another five minutes. Once caramelized, remove from heat and refrigerate until use.

DATE KETCHUP

YIELD: 3 ½ CUPS

1 tsp. olive oil

1 small yellow onion, minced

2 cups Medjool dates, pitted

2 cups ketchup

1 cup beer

Heat olive oil in a small pan over medium heat. Add onions and sauté. Add dates, ketchup, and beer. Reduce heat to low and simmer for 25 minutes. Remove from heat, cool slightly, then purée in blender. Keep refrigerated until use.

PICKLED JALAPEÑOS

YIELD: 1 ⅓ CUPS

2 cups white vinegar
1 cup water
1 tsp. mustard seeds
1 T. sugar
12 medium jalapeño peppers, stems and seeds discarded, diced
1 yellow onion, thinly sliced
3 garlic cloves, thinly sliced

In a small pot, gently warm vinegar, water, mustard seeds, and sugar. Place jalapeños, onions, and garlic in a glass jar. Cover with liquid, cool, then refrigerate for up to three months.

MARROW BUTTER

YIELD: 18 OUNCES, ENOUGH FOR 8 – 10 STEAKS

CHEF TIP
Blending the butter and marrow with your hands makes it easier to emulsify. This is great on steaks!

4 6" beef bones (have your butcher cut in half lengthwise)
1 lb. butter, room temperature
4 shallots, minced
12 sprigs thyme, chopped
salt & pepper

Scoop out marrow from bone. Combine in bowl with butter. Add shallots, thyme, salt and pepper. Refrigerate or freeze half until ready to use.

QUICK PICKLED CUKES

YIELD: 2 CUPS

2 English cucumbers, sliced in half lengthwise
1 cup rice wine vinegar
½ cup Thai sweet chili sauce
⅓ cup sugar

Remove seeds from cucumbers, slice ¼" on a bias. In a bowl, combine sliced cucumbers, rice wine vinegar, sweet chili sauce, and sugar. Place into a jar with a lid, refrigerate and reserve until ready to use. Will last up to six weeks.

BASIL MAYO

YIELD: 1 ½ CUPS

CHEF TIP
There's a huge difference between good and bad mayo. I use Hellmann's.

1 large handful fresh basil
1 cup mayonnaise
1 clove garlic, chopped
salt to taste

Purée ingredients in blender. Season to taste. Refrigerate.

HARISSA MAYO

YIELD: 1 CUPS

1 T. harissa paste
1 cup mayonnaise
1 tsp. sugar
salt to taste

Whisk all ingredients together in a bowl. Refrigerate.

JERK MAYO

YIELD: 1 CUP

1 cup mayonnaise
1 T. jerk seasoning
3 dashes Worcestershire
1 T. water

Whisk all ingredients together. Refrigerate.

GARLIC THYME AIOLI

YIELD: 1 ½ CUPS

10 whole garlic cloves
1 cup olive oil
1 T. fresh chopped thyme leaves
3 egg yolks
salt to taste

Place garlic cloves and olive oil in saucepan over low heat for 20 minutes or until the garlic is soft. Remove garlic from oil, purée with thyme in blender. Add egg yolks and blend. Add olive oil and 1 T. water from pan slowly until emulsified. Season to taste.

DEMI-GLACE

YIELD: 1 QUART

CHEF TIP

To reduce cloudiness in stock, separate two eggs, reserving yolks for another use. Whisk whites with 2 teaspoons cold water and add to simmering stock during the end of the second cooking process, after it has been strained and reduced. Turn off heat. As the egg whites cook, they act as a raft, removing impurities, and rising to the surface for easy skimming.

5 lb. veal or beef bones

¾ cup olive oil

salt to taste

1 bunch celery, chopped

12 garlic cloves

3 medium yellow onions, chopped

3 carrots, chopped

2 cups red wine

4 tomatoes, quartered

6 sprigs thyme

2 bay leaves

10 peppercorns

Preheat oven to 400 degrees. In roasting pan, toss bones in ½ cup olive oil and salt. Roast for 25 – 30 minutes or until crispy and caramelized. Remove from pan and set aside.

Meanwhile, in large stockpot, sauté celery, garlic, onion, and carrots in ¼ cup olive oil. Add red wine to roasting pan, place over a medium-high flame, and cook 3 minutes to deglaze. Add to vegetables in stockpot. Add bones. Cover with the water. Add tomatoes, thyme, bay leaves, and peppercorns. Cook over medium heat until reduced by half, about 3 hours.

Strain, removing bones and vegetables. Cook remaining liquid over medium-low heat to reduce by half, about 2 hours. Refrigerate.

POUTINE GRAVY

YIELD: 4 CUPS

12 oz. butter

1 cup all-purpose flour

2 cups chicken stock

8 oz. heavy cream

salt & pepper to taste

In large saucepan over medium heat, melt butter. Stir in flour and cook until roux is toasted, about 2 – 3 minutes. Whisk in stock, then cream. Cook 10 minutes, continuing to stir until thickened. Season with salt.

COUNTRY GRAVY

YIELD: 2 CUPS

6 oz. butter

6 oz. ground pork or breakfast sausage

½ cup all-purpose flour

1 ½ cups chicken stock

4 oz. heavy cream

salt & pepper to taste

In large saucepan over medium heat, melt butter. Add pork sausage to brown. Remove sausage, leaving the fat in the pan. Stir in flour and cook until roux is toasted, about 2 – 3 minutes. Whisk in stock, then cream. Cook 10 minutes, continuing to stir until thickened. Season with salt and pepper.

BEER CHEESE

YIELD: 3 CUPS

8 oz. American cheese, unsliced
8 oz. heavy cream
8 oz. IPA beer

Combine ingredients in saucepan over low heat, stirring constantly until heated through.

VARIATIONS

SLIM JIM BEER CHEESE
Add 2 finely chopped Slim Jims to recipe above.

ROASTED POBLANO BEER CHEESE
Add 1 large poblano pepper, roasted, seeded, and chopped to recipe above.

KENTUCKY BOURBON BARREL ALE CHEESE
Substitute ale for IPA.

CHIPOTLE BEER CHEESE
Stir in 3 tablespoons of seeded, chopped, canned chipotles in adobo sauce to recipe above.

CHEF TIP
Great with warm bread, on nachos, or in a bread bowl.

BROWN SUGAR PEANUT SAUCE

YIELD: 1 ½ CUPS

2 T. brown sugar
3 oz. peanut butter
6 oz. Thai sweet chile sauce
1 tsp. sriracha sauce
8 sprigs cilantro, leaves removed and chopped

In a mixing bowl, whisk all ingredients together.

REFRIED BEANS

SERVES 8 - 10

1 ½ lb. pinto or black beans, soaked in water overnight
1 small red onion, chopped
2 tsp. garlic, minced
2 T. extra virgin olive oil
1 quart chicken stock
2 T. butter

Strain beans. Sauté onions and garlic in olive oil; add beans. Cover with stock and cook until soft but not mushy, approximately 1 hour. Strain. Mash beans. Melt butter in sauté pan and cook mashed beans until crisped.

VARIATIONS

BACON FAT BEANS

Instead of butter, heat ½ cup bacon fat plus 1 teaspoon Tabasco sauce in a pan. Add beans and cook 5 minutes.

CHORIZO REFRIED BEANS

Over medium heat, brown 1 pound chorizo (page 172) in 1 ounce olive oil. Add beans and cook for 5 minutes.

CRISPY FRIED TORTILLA STRIPS

YIELD: 2 CUPS, ENOUGH FOR 6 – 8 DOGS

1 quart vegetable oil or shortening
6 soft corn tortillas, sliced into thin strips
salt to taste

In a 2-quart pot, heat oil or shortening to 350 degrees. Carefully add tortilla strips to hot oil. Fry until golden brown, about two minutes. Remove and place on a paper towel-lined plate. Season with salt.

CRISPY FRIED ONIONS

YIELD: 4 CUPS

1 quart vegetable oil or shortening

2 eggs + ¼ cup water for egg wash

2 medium red onions, peeled, cut in half and sliced into ¼" pieces

2 cups all-purpose flour, seasoned with salt & pepper

salt to taste

In a 2-quart pot, heat oil or shortening to 350 degrees. Toss onions into egg wash then into flour. Shake off excess flour and carefully add to oil. Fry until golden brown, about 2 minutes. Remove and drain on a paper towel. Season with salt.

VARIATION

BACON FAT FRIED ONIONS

Toss crispy onions with a tablespoon of applewood smoked bacon drippings. After frying, drain on paper towel. Season with salt.

CHIPOTLE CREMA

YIELD: 3 CUPS

3 ½ oz. chipotles in adobo sauce (about half a can)

2 cups sour cream or crème fraîche

¼ cup milk

salt to taste

Remove peppers and reserve adobo sauce. Remove seeds from peppers. In a blender, add crème fraîche or sour cream, seeded chipotles, reserved adobo sauce, and milk. Blend and season with salt. If you would like the crema less spicy, then add half the amount of peppers and sauce.

APPLE CIDER BALLPARK MUSTARD

YIELD: 1 CUP

2 cups apple cider vinegar
1 tsp. sugar
3 T. ballpark or Dusseldorf mustard

In a small non-aluminum pan over medium heat, reduce cider vinegar by half. Stir in sugar and mustard. Refrigerate.

CILANTRO YOGURT

YIELD: 2 CUPS

2 cups Greek yogurt
½ cup cream or milk
1 bunch cilantro, leaves removed
juice of 1 lime
salt to taste

In a blender, purée yogurt, cream, cilantro, and lime juice. Season with salt. Refrigerate.

BALSAMIC GLAZE

YIELD: 1 CUP

3 cups balsamic vinegar
3 T. sugar

Combine ingredients in non-aluminum saucepan. Cook over low heat until reduced by two thirds, approximately 20 – 30 minutes. Remove and chill.

ROASTED MUSHROOM & POBLANO SALSA

YIELD: 3 CUPS

3 portobello mushrooms, stems removed
1 poblano pepper
1 red onion, peeled and sliced into thick rounds
3 T. olive oil
1 medium tomato, chopped
1 bunch cilantro, chopped
2 T. champagne vinegar
juice of 2 limes
salt to taste

Heat grill to high. Toss mushrooms, poblano, and onion slices with 1 tablespoon of olive oil. Grill until mushrooms are tender, onions are charred, and pepper is blistered. Cool. Remove skin from pepper; de-seed and chop. Chop mushrooms and onions into uniform dice; stir together with pepper, tomato, cilantro, vinegar, lime juice, and remaining olive oil. Season with salt.

HONEY DIJON

YIELD: 1 ⅓ CUPS

1 cup Dijon mustard
⅓ cup wild honey

In a small bowl, stir ingredients until blended. Refrigerate.

COLESLAW

YIELD: 4 CUPS

3 cups cabbage, shredded
1 cup purple cabbage, shredded
1 cup carrot, peeled and grated
1 ½ cups mayonnaise
2 T. water
3 T. sugar
salt to taste

Combine shredded cabbages and carrots in a bowl. Add mayonnaise, water, and sugar. Season with salt. Refrigerate.

REMOULADE

YIELD: 2 CUPS

1 T. olive oil
1 small red onion, chopped
1 cup homemade pickles (page 27) or your favorite bread and butter pickles, chopped
1 small bunch flat leaf parsley, chopped
1 ½ cups mayonnaise
2 T. sriracha sauce
¼ cup ketchup
juice of half fresh lime
salt & pepper to taste

In a small sauté pan, add olive oil and sauté red onions until caramelized. Mix pickles, parsley, and onions together in a bowl. Stir in mayo, sriracha, ketchup, and lime juice. Season with salt and pepper. Refrigerate.

ROASTED BANANA DIJON

YIELD: 1 ½ CUPS

2 ripe bananas
1 tsp. sugar
1 cup Dijon mustard
salt to taste

Preheat oven to 350 degrees. Roast bananas 10 minutes or until caramelized. Remove from pan and purée in blender with sugar and Dijon. Season with salt. Refrigerate.

CARROT & DAIKON SLAW

YIELD: 2 CUPS

1 large carrot, peeled
1 small daikon, peeled
1 cup mirin
5 sprigs cilantro, leaves removed
1 T. sugar

Slice carrot and daikon on mandoline ⅛" thick, then julienne into matchstick. Mix with rest of ingredients. Refrigerate.

KITTEN FIZZ

YIELD: 1 COCKTAIL

5 raspberries
½ oz. simple syrup
¾ oz. Tito's Vodka
¾ oz. St. Germain
1 ½ oz. club soda

In a collins glass, muddle 3 raspberries in simple syrup. Add vodka, St. Germain, soda, and ice. Garnish with remaining berries.

Feel free to go wild here and substitute peaches, blueberries, blackberries, or strawberries for raspberries.

STREET CAR

YIELD: 1 COCKTAIL

1 oz. walnut-infused cognac (recipe follows)
½ oz. apricot brandy
2 bourbon amaretto cherries (recipe follows)
lemon twist
soda water, optional

WALNUT-INFUSED COGNAC
YIELD: 22 OUNCES, ENOUGH FOR 20 COCKTAILS

Toast ½ cup of walnuts in a 375 degree oven for 5 minutes or until lightly browned. Add walnuts and a 750 ml bottle of cognac to an airtight, nonreactive container. Store at room temperature for 4 days, shaking occasionally. Strain through a fine-mesh sieve and pour back into bottle. Keeps in the refrigerator for a month.

BOURBON AMARETTO CHERRIES
YIELD: 50 CHERRIES

1 lb. frozen sweet black cherries
1 ½ cups bourbon
½ cup amaretto
1 T. cardamom pods, cracked

Mix all ingredients in a glass jar. Refrigerate. Allow to marinate at least 24 hours.

In a rocks glass, pour cognac and brandy over ice and stir. Garnish with cherries and a twist. Optional: Top with a splash of soda.

MR. CHOW

YIELD: 1 COCKTAIL

¾ oz. Chin Chin Thai Basil Seed Drink
1 oz. browned butter-infused rum (recipe follows)
½ oz. Frangelico
¾ oz. Velvet Falernum
½ oz. fresh lime juice
1 oz. pineapple juice
bourbon amaretto cherry (page 197)
orange slice

DRINK TIP

Pick up a can of Chin Chin at your local Asian market, or make your own by soaking a heaping tablespoon of Thai basil seeds in 2 cups water plus 1 tablespoon honey, or more to taste. Within minutes, they expand, forming a jelly-like coating that snap, crackle, and pop when you bite down on them.

BROWNED BUTTER-INFUSED RUM

YIELD: 24 OUNCES

Brown 2 ounces butter in a skillet over low heat. Remove from heat. Carefully stir in a 750 ml bottle of Bacardi Silver. Place in an airtight container at room temperature for 24 hours. Move to freezer for 12 hours. Skim off solidified butter from the top. Strain rum through a fine-mesh sieve and bottle.

In a collins glass, pour Chin Chin Thai Basil drink over crushed ice. Place remaining ingredients except for cherries and orange into cocktail shaker over ice; shake well and strain into the glass. Stir. Garnish with bourbon amaretto cherry and orange slice.

LUCY LOU

YIELD: 1 COCKTAIL

¾ oz. limoncello (recipe follows)
¾ oz. St. Germain
½ oz. fresh squeezed lemon juice
1 ½ oz. champagne or sparkling white wine
lemon twist

> ### LIMONCELLO
> **YIELD:** 8 CUPS
>
> Peel 10 – 15 lemons. Place the peels in a 2 ½-quart pitcher. Pour a 750 ml bottle of vodka over the peels and cover with plastic wrap. Steep the lemon peels in the vodka for 1 week to 2 months in a dark place at room temperature.
>
> Stir 4 cups water and 4 cups sugar in a large saucepan over medium heat until the sugar dissolves, about 5 minutes. Cool completely. Pour the sugar syrup over the vodka mixture until desired sweetness. Cover and let stand at room temperature overnight. Strain the limoncello through a fine-mesh strainer. Discard the peels.

In a cocktail shaker, combine limoncello, St. Germain, and lemon juice over ice. Shake and strain into champagne flute. Fill with champagne and top with a twist.

RUMSPRINGA PUNCH

YIELD: 16 COCKTAILS

16 oz. cucumber tarragon-infused rum (recipe follows)
16 oz. hibiscus-infused pineapple juice (recipe follows)
8 oz. Domaine de Canton (ginger-flavored liqueur)
8 oz. fresh squeezed lime juice
4 oz. simple syrup
16 oz. champagne or sparkling white wine
hibiscus flowers

DRINK TIP

The hibiscus flowers lend this punch its gorgeous purple hue and zang of tart cranberry. Purchase them dried in bulk at Asian markets, or preserved in syrup from stores such as Whole Foods, Kroger, or Williams-Sonoma.

CUCUMBER TARRAGON-INFUSED RUM
YIELD: 28 OUNCES

Pour a 750 ml bottle of Bacardi Silver into an airtight container. Add 3 sprigs of tarragon and one cucumber, thinly sliced. After 24 hours, strain through a fine-mesh sieve and bottle.

HIBISCUS-INFUSED PINEAPPLE JUICE
YIELD: 2 CUPS

In a bowl, add 2 packets of hibiscus tea to 2 cups of pineapple juice. Stir and let sit for 30 minutes. Remove tea packets.

Pour all ingredients except for champagne into a punch bowl over ice. Ladle into coupe glass. Top each glass with an ounce of champagne and garnish with a hibiscus flower.

ICHABOD CRANE

YIELD: 1 COCKTAIL

apple cider ice cube
1 T. pumpkin butter
1 ½ oz. applejack brandy
½ oz. Domaine de Canton (ginger-flavored liqueur)
6 drops chili pepper tincture (recipe follows)
2 oz. Hefeweizen (German wheat beer)

DRINK TIP

In addition to the Hefeweizen, we love this cocktail with a regional favorite, Kentucky Bourbon Barrel Ale, a smooth and robust sipping beer with notes of vanilla and char.

CHILI PEPPER TINCTURE

YIELD: 6 – 8 OUNCES

Remove seeds from 4 chili peppers and macerate along with another whole pepper (seeds included) in 6 ounces of high proof, neutral spirit grain alcohol for 24 – 48 hours. Strain through a fine-mesh sieve and bottle.

Place apple cider ice cube into glass. In a cocktail shaker, combine pumpkin butter, brandy, Domaine de Canton, and chili pepper tincture over ice. Shake and strain into snifter, fill with beer.

POOTY TANG

YIELD: 1 COCKTAIL

1 ¾ oz. spiced rum
½ oz. Domaine de Canton (ginger-flavored liqueur)
¾ oz. ginger syrup (recipe follows)
2 oz. carrot juice
½ oz. fresh lime juice
2 dashes celery bitters (we love The Bitter Truth brand)
1 dehydrated kiwi slice

DRINK TIP

Fee Brothers is a fine brand of celery bitters, but we love the complexity of The Bitter Truth. Which is always better than the sweetest lie.

GINGER SYRUP

YIELD: 2 CUPS

Boil 6 ounces sliced fresh gingerroot in 2 cups water for 15 minutes. Add 2 cups sugar. Stir until dissolved. Strain through a fine-mesh sieve and bottle.

In a collins glass, combine all ingredients over ice. Stir and garnish with kiwi slice.

"Working with really talented, passionate people fuels my creativity."

Mike Georgitan (aka Seabass),
Senate Bar Manager

HONEY ON YOUR STINGER

YIELD: 1 COCKTAIL

1 ¼ oz. Wild Turkey American Honey

½ oz. Grand Marnier

½ oz. Domaine de Canton (ginger-flavored liqueur)

½ oz. Punt E Mes (Italian vermouth)

2 oz. Kentucky Bourbon Barrel Ale

Place 1 large ice cube in a rocks glass or snifter. Combine Wild Turkey, Grand Marnier, Domaine de Canton, and Punt E Mes in a cocktail shaker over ice. Stir and strain into glass. Fill with ale.

Carpano Punt E Mes is a deeply flavored, bittersweet red vermouth with forward notes of dried fruit that yield to herbs and spices before finishing dry and bitter. Once you've opened it, keep refrigerated.

IT'S PERSONAL

1442 Chestnut St., Apt. #1.
The address where an unpolished cook from Chicago and an inexperienced photographer from Green Bay would meet, become friends, painstakingly grow up, eventually get their shit together, and even meet their future wives. During booze-soaked late nights, we talked about our futures, agreeing that if both of us ever "made it"—meaning if people gave a shit about my food and if he could learn how to hold a camera—that one day we'd do a cookbook together.

It's been twelve years since that apartment in Chicago. I've watched Tony grow into an incredible father and businessman, as well as a creative force with a camera. Though we both have busted ass to accomplish our goals, I don't think either of us imagined then that this small pipe dream would ever really come to fruition. But here it is—a cookbook that is more than the sum of its parts, something far more personal.

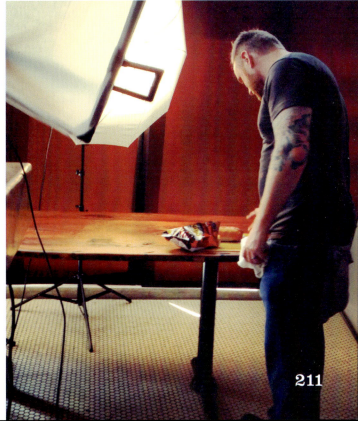

FIDEL CASTRO

YIELD: 1 COCKTAIL

2 oz. oak-aged spiced rum (recipe follows)
½ oz. pure maple syrup
3 dashes Angostura bitters
1 dash orange bitters
1" piece of orange peel

DRINK TIP

We barrel age our homemade spiced rum 4–6 months using a Buffalo Trace bourbon barrel. Smaller barrels can be purchased online, or try adding oak chips (French or American) straight to the mixture after first soaking them in bourbon (24–48 hours should do the trick). If you don't have the patience for six months, we recommend you wait at least a week before dipping in to it.

HOMEMADE SPICED RUM

YIELD: 1.75 liters

750 ml bottle Bacardi Silver Rum
1 vanilla bean, halved lengthwise
2 whole cinnamon sticks
1 T. whole coriander, cracked
10 allspice berries, cracked
3 black peppercorns, cracked
2 whole nutmegs, cracked
1 ½ tsp. whole cloves
1 T. cardamom pods, cracked
1 star anise
1 T. sarsaparilla bark or root (optional)
3 4" x 1" strips orange peel, white pith removed
5 slices gingerroot
¼ cup French or American oak chips

Combine ingredients in a large glass jar. Cover and allow to age, shaking every few days. We age ours 6 months, but can be used after a few days.

Place one large ice cube in a rocks glass. Combine all ingredients except orange peel over ice in a cocktail shaker. Stir and strain into glass. Heat up orange peel with a lighter. Squeeze the peel over the glass, rubbing the rim with it before adding it to cocktail.

SCISSOR FIGHT

YIELD: 1 COCKTAIL

1 ½ oz. vanilla vodka
½ oz. Cointreau
½ oz. pistachio syrup (page 217)
1 tsp. peach butter
pinch of cinnamon
1 oz. Riesling

Combine all ingredients except Riesling in a cocktail shaker over ice. Shake and strain into champagne flute. Top with Riesling.

COUP DE GRAS

YIELD: 1 COCKTAIL

2 oz. foie gras-infused cognac (recipe follows)
⅛ oz. black pepper tincture (recipe follows)
1 T. sauternes and fig emulsion (recipe follows)
½ oz. pistachio syrup (recipe follows)
sprinkle of nutmeg

FOIE GRAS-INFUSED COGNAC
YIELD: 23 OUNCES

Finely chop 3 ounces of foie gras lobe. Cook over medium heat until most of foie gras has liquefied. Remove from heat. Carefully add a 750 ml bottle of cognac to skillet, stir gently. Place in an airtight container at room temperature for 24 hours. Move to freezer for 12 hours. Strain through a fine-mesh sieve and bottle. Keep refrigerated.

BLACK PEPPER TINCTURE
YIELD: 6 OUNCES

Place 1 tablespoon of black peppercorns in 6 ounces of a high proof, neutral spirit grain alcohol for 24 – 48 hours. Strain through a fine-mesh sieve and bottle.

SAUTERNES AND FIG EMULSION
YIELD: 2 CUPS

Slice 12 figs. Blend with 8 ounces of sauternes in a blender until smooth.

PISTACHIO SYRUP
YIELD: 3 CUPS

Crush ½ cup of pistachios. Boil in 2 cups water for 10 minutes. Add 2 cups sugar; stir until dissolved. Remove from heat, chill. Strain through a fine-mesh sieve and bottle.

Combine all ingredients except nutmeg in a cocktail shaker; fill with ice. Shake and strain into a coupe glass. Sprinkle with nutmeg.

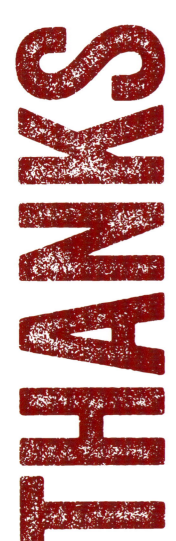

DANIEL & LANA WRIGHT

Thank you to our family and friends. To our sons, who remind us every day how beautiful life is. Our parents for their love, support, and for telling us the truth about life—even if it isn't always pretty. To our brothers and sisters for supporting us throughout this journey in more ways than we can count. Stephen, Adam, Chad, and the team over at 3CDC for giving us the opportunity to build our dream. To Tracey and our Angel Investor. It still touches us to think that you helped us in such a way. We don't think we could ever pay you back, we just hope one day we can pay it forward. To our staff, our staff, and our staff, thank you for everything you do. To all our customers and supporters who have been so amazingly kind and loyal. Thank you! Courtney, Donna, Kelly, Stephanie, and Tony, we can't thank you enough for all the hours, passion, and dedication you've poured into this project. Without you, this would be nothing more than a hot dog coloring book.

COURTNEY TSITOURIS

To Dustin, for walking through the fire. To Donna, my editor and partner, for your magic wand and wicked humor. Thanks, Tim Quinlivan, for taking a chance on me. Love to mom, dad, Marin, and the gingers for keeping me sane. To Kelly Pennington, who burned the midnight oil on this one, for your patience and uproarious laughter even in hard times. To Dan and Lana for this wild ride, for your fearlessness and good faith. To the people with knives—kitchen wenches, home cooks, butchers, and bohemians. You inspire me. Rock on.

DONNA COVRETT

To my love doctor, Doug, who nearly had a heart attack the day I announced I was leaving my career in magazine journalism to start a company whose first project was a book about hot dogs—and supported me anyway. To my willing accomplice Courtney—the Larry to my Balki and the Shirley to my Laverne. To Dan and Lana for their fierce attention to detail, an essential tool whether creating a restaurant or a book.

KELLY PENNINGTON

To Dan Wright, whose story and food makes me weep. To Courtney Tsitouris, future ruler of the world, it's been a crazy ride (Rufus forever)! To Tom Crusham for spending the last seventeen years making me a better designer. To my peeps, Laurie, Kristi, Jen, Kristy, Julie, Steph and Karen for your friendship. To my furry baby, Suki, for always being happy to see me. Thanks to my family; we're weird, but we always stick together. To my stepmother, Jummy, for being my "other" mother for the last thirty-six years. To my parents, James and Charlotte Pennington, I miss you both every day. Most of all thanks to my twin sister, Kim, who was put on this earth to make me a better person.

ANTHONY TAHLIER

To my sweetie pie wife, Andrea – my support since there has been an us and inventor of my favorite people on earth.

Aioli
Garlic Thyme, 181:
Mc Schnitzel, 141
Red Pepper, 99:
Sarah Jessica Porker, 98
Scallion Miso, Charred, 118:
Captain Jenkins, 118

Apple
Bacon Relish, 95
Fennel Sausage, 173
Slaw, Celery Root, 156
Cider:
Ichabod Crane, 205

Arugula
Goetta Superstar, 74
Lindsey Lowhan, 82
My Wife's Salad, 134
Silence of the Lamb, 60

Avocado
Guacamole, 176
My Wife's Salad, 134
Una Noche con Nick Lachey, 85

Bacon
Advice, 9
Apple, Relish, 95
Beans, Bacon Fat, 186
Captain Jenkins, 118
Elvis, 105
Fries, Bacon Fat, 24
Grilled Peach Salad, 128
Hello Kitty Dog, 77
Jesse Spano, 69
Just in B Bear, 68
Lindsey Lowhan, 82
Lobster BLT, 159
Mexico City, 70
Natalie Porkman, 107
Okra Winfrey, 81
Onions, Bacon Fat Fried, 187
Prince Harry, 109
Salad, and Egg, 145
Scallops, Leeks & Salsify, 150
Trailer Park, 55
White Trash Wedding, 91
Country Fried, 28:
Honey Boo Boo, 100

Banana
Elvis, 105
Roasted, Dijon, 191

Basil
Jersey Shore, 108
Mayo, 180
Tomato, Eggplant & Onion Relish, 108

BBQ
Pork Belly, BBQ, 169:
Booty & Belly, 156
Boss Hog, 84
Senate, Sauce, 177:
BBQ Pork Belly, 169
Booty & Belly, 156
Just in B Bear, 68
Pig Tails, 125
White Trash Wedding, 91

Beans
Bacon Fat, 186
Refried, 186:
Prince Harry, 109
Refried, Chorizo, 186:
Nacho Man Randy Savage, 114

Béchamel, 71
Croque Madame, 71

Beef *see also* Veal
Bone Marrow, 42
Demi-glace, 182
Lamb Burger, 155
Marrow Butter, 179
Merguez Sausage, 173
Senate Burger, 160
Slim Jim Beer Cheese, 185
Substitutions, 53
Short Ribs, Braised, 166; 8, 59, 165:
Cabo, 101
Korean, 59
Poutine, 133
Poutine Dog, 92
Short Ribs, Curried, 167; 166:
Bollywood, 117

Beer
Beer Cheese(s), 185
Braised Pork Belly, 168
Date Ketchup, 178
Honey on Your Stinger, 209
Ichabod Crane, 205
Onion Rings, 35
Senate BBQ Sauce, 177

Bell Pepper, Red
Pork Fennel Sausage, 172
Red Pepper Aioli, 99
Tomato, Eggplant & Onion Relish, 108

Bourbon
Amaretto Cherries, 197
Honey on Your Stinger, 209

Brandy
Cognac, Foie Gras-infused, 216
Cognac, Walnut-infused, 197
Coup de Gras, 216
Foie Gras Torchon, 140
Honey on Your Stinger, 209

Ichabod Crane, 205
Street Car, 197

Bratwurst, 173
Brat Michaels, 94
Natalie Porkman, 107

Cabbage
Coleslaw, 190
Ponzu-Wasabi Slaw, 77

Carrot
Braised Beef Short Ribs, 166
Braised Pork Belly, 168
Coleslaw, 190
Demi-glace, 182
Ponzu-Wasabi Slaw, 77
Pooty Tang, 206
Slaw, Daikon, 191

Champagne
Lucy Lou, 201
Rumspringa Punch, 202

Charmoula Sauce, 148; 147
Mussels, 148

Cheese
American:
Béchamel, 71
Beer Cheese, 185
Lobster Mac 'n Cheese, 32
Trailer Park, 55
Beer Cheese, 185; 31:
White Trash Wedding, 91
Beer Cheese, Chipotle, 185:
Natalie Porkman, 107
Beer Cheese, Kentucky Bourbon Barrel Ale, 185:
Boss Hog, 84
Beer Cheese, Roasted Poblano, 185:
Prince Harry, 109
Beer Cheese, Slim Jim, 185:
Nacho Man Randy Savage, 114
Cheddar:
Jesse Spano, 69
Senate Burger, 160
Curd, 38:
Poutine, 133
Poutine Dog, 92
Curds, Fried, 38; 118:
Captain Jenkins, 118
Feta:
Jimmy the Greek, 56
Goat:
Grilled Peach Salad, 128
Just in B Bear, 68
Lamb Burger, 155
Lindsey Lowhan, 82
Silence of the Lamb, 60
Mozzarella:
Jersey Shore, 108
My Wife's Salad, 134

Queso Fresco:
Cabo, 101
Una Noche con Nick Lachey, 85
Swiss:
Cuban, 88

Cherry
Bourbon Amaretto, 197
Mr. Chow, 198
Preserves, 138
Street Car, 197

Chicken
Substitutions, 53
Jerk Sausage, 173:
Madame Cleo, 93
Stock:
Braised Pork Belly, 168
Charmoula Sauce, 148
Country Gravy, 184
Poutine Gravy, 184
Refried Beans, 186

Chickpea
Sweet Potato Falafel, 139

Chili Pepper
Hot Sauce, 41
Tincture, 205

Chipotle
Beer Cheese, 185
Senate BBQ Sauce, 177
Crema, 187:
Cabo, 101
Green Corn Tamale, 142
Mexico City, 70
Una Noche con Nick Lachey, 85

Chorizo, 172
Prince Harry, 109
Refried Beans, 186

Chutney, Mango, 117
Bollywood, 117

Cilantro
Apple Celery Root Slaw, 156
Bollywood, 117
Brown Sugar Peanut Sauce, 185
Carrot & Daikon Slaw, 191
Charmoula Sauce, 148
Ginger Pork Sausage, 172
Guacamole, 176
Mango Chutney, 117
Mayo, 98
Mussels Charmoula, 148
One Night in Bangkok, 63
Pico de Gallo, 114
Pig Tails, 125
Prince Harry, 109
Roasted Mushroom & Poblano Salsa, 189

Salsa Verde, 70
Sweet Corn Country Relish, 98
Sweet Potato Falafel, 139
Una Noche con Nick Lachey, 85
Yogurt, 188

Cocktails
Coup de Gras, 216
Fidel Castro, 212
Honey on Your Stinger, 209
Ichabod Crane, 205
Kitten Fizz, 194
Lucy Lou, 201
Mr. Chow, 198
Pooty Tang, 206
Scissor Fight, 215
Street Car, 197
Rumspringa Punch, 202

Coleslaw, *see* Slaw

Corn
Green, Tamale, 142
Relish, Sweet, Butternut, 100
Relish, Sweet, Country, 98

Cranberry
Jam, Shallot, 42
Mango Chutney, 117

Cream Cheese, 68
Miso, 122:
Potstickers, 122

Cucumber, *see also* Pickles
Cukes, Quick Pickled, 180
Lemony Tzatziki, 56
Tarragon-infused, Rum, 202

Cukes, *see also* Pickles
Homemade Pickles, 27
Quick Pickled, 180:
Korean, 59
One Night in Bangkok, 63

Curry
Mango Chutney, 117
Short Ribs, 167

Daikon
Slaw, Carrot, 191

Dates
Ketchup, 178

Demi-glace, 182
Braised Beef Short Ribs, 166

Dijon, *see also* Mustard
Balsamic Vinaigrette, 134
Mc Schnitzel, 141
Senate Burger, 160

Shallot Cranberry Jam, 42
Sweet Corn Butternut Relish, 100
Brown Sugar, 94:
Brat Michaels, 94
Honey, 189; 141:
Honey Boo Boo, 100
Roasted Banana, 191:
Cuban, 88
Elvis, 105

Dressing
Balsamic Vinaigrette, 134:
My Wife's Salad, 134
Buttermilk Tarragon, 176; 31, 35:
Grilled Peach Salad, 128
Madame Cleo, 93
Tarragon Vinaigrette, 145:
Bacon and Egg Salad, 145

Duck
Fries, Duck Fat, 24
Foie Gras:
Cognac, infused 216
Torchon, 140; 8:
Elvis, 105
It's Brittany, 104
PBJ&F, 138

Egg
Croque Madame, 71
Goetta Superstar, 74
Poutine, 133
Poutine Dog, 92
Salad, and Bacon, 145
Sarah Jessica Porker, 98

Eggplant
Relish, Tomato, Onion, 108

Encased Meat, 172, 173; 9, 53

Falafel, Sweet Potato, 139

Fennel
Sausage, Pork Apple, 173
Sausage, Pork, 172

Fig
Emulsion, Sauternes, 217
Relish, Black Mission, 60

Fries, 24; 140
Advice, 9
Bacon Fat, 24
Duck Fat, 24
Truffle, 24:
Poutine, 133
Poutine Dog, 92

Gingerroot
Champagne Mignonette, 41
Ginger Pork Sausage, 172
Pig Tails, 125

Syrup, 206:
Pooty Tang, 206

Goetta, 173
Goetta Superstar, 74

Gravy
Country, 184; 28:
Goetta Superstar, 74
Poutine, 184:
Poutine, 133
Poutine Dog, 92

Grippo's BAR-B-Q Chips
Trailer Park, 55

Guacamole, 176
Cabo, 101
Mexico City, 70

Gyro Meat
Jimmy the Greek, 56

Ham
Andouille Sausage, 172
Croque Madame, 71
Cuban, 88
Sweet Corn Country Relish, 98

Harissa
Mayo, 180

Hibiscus
Juice, Infused Pineapple, 202
Rumspringa Punch, 202
Tea, 202

Honey
Brown Sugar Dijon, 94
Dijon, 189
Elvis, 105
Sweet Corn Butternut Relish, 100

Hot Dogs
Advice, 9; 7
Bollywood, 117; 59, 166
Boss Hog, 84
Brat Michaels, 94
Cabo, 101; 59
Captain Jenkins, 118
Croque Madame, 71
Cuban, 88
Elvis, 105; 140
Goetta Superstar, 74
Hello Kitty Dog, 77; 52
Honey Boo Boo, 100; 52
It's Brittany, 104; 140
Jersey Shore, 108
Jesse Spano, 69
Jimmy the Greek, 56
Just in B Bear, 68

221

Korean, 59; 165
Lindsey Lowhan, 82
Madame Cleo, 93
Mexico City, 70
Nacho Man Randy Savage, 114
Natalie Porkman, 107; 44
Okra Winfrey, 81
One Night in Bangkok, 63
Poutine Dog, 92; 59
Prince Harry, 109
Sarah Jessica Porker, 98
Silence of the Lamb, 60
Substitutions, 53
Trailer Park, 55; 7
Una Noche con Nick Lachey, 85
White Trash Wedding, 91

Hot Sauce, 41
Oysters, 41

Jalapeño
Black Mission Fig Relish, 60
Guacamole, 176
Mango Chutney, 117
Pico de Gallo, 114
Pickled, 179:
Nacho Man Randy Savage, 114
Una Noche con Nick Lachey, 85

Jam
Shallot Cranberry, 42:
Bone Marrow, 42

Jerk
Chicken Sausage, 173
Mayo, 181

Ketchup
Senate BBQ Sauce, 177
Date, 178; 35:
Lamb Burger, 155

Kimchi
Korean, 59

Lamb
Burger, 155
Substitutions, 53
Merguez Sausage, 173:
Silence of the Lamb, 60

Leek
Scallops, Salsify, 150

Lemon
Limoncello, 201
Lucy Lou, 201
Oysters, 41
Preserves, 138
Tzatziki, 56

Lettuce, Greens
Bacon and Egg Salad, 145
Grilled Peach Salad, 128
It's Brittany, 104
Mc Schnitzel, 141
Lamb Burger, 155
Lobster BLT, 159
Senate Burger, 160
Sweet Potato Falafel, 139

Lime
Black Mission Fig Relish, 60
Cilantro Yogurt, 188
Guacamole, 176
Mango Chutney, 117
Mr. Chow, 198
Pico de Gallo, 114
Pooty Tang, 206
Roasted Mushroom
 & Poblano Salsa, 189
Rumspringa Punch, 202
Salsa Verde, 70
Wasabi Mayonnaise, 177

Liqueur
Bourbon Amaretto Cherries, 197
Honey on Your Stinger, 209
Ichabod Crane, 205
Kitten Fizz, 194
Limoncello, 201
Lucy Lou, 201
Mr. Chow, 198
Pooty Tang, 206
Rumspringa Punch, 202
Scissor Fight, 215

Lobster
BLT, 159
Mac 'n Cheese, 32

Mango
Chutney, 117

Maple Syrup
Brown Sugar Pork Sausage, 172
Fidel Castro, 212

Marrow
Bone, 42
Butter, 179

Mayonnaise
Apple Celery Root Slaw, 156
Buttermilk Tarragon Dressing, 176
Charred Scallion Miso Aioli, 118
Coleslaw, 190
Jerk, 181
Red Pepper Aioli, 99
Remoulade, 190

Basil, 180; 98:
Lobster BLT, 159
Harissa, 180:
Korean, 59
Senate Burger, 160
Wasabi, 177:
Hello Kitty Dog, 77
Ponzu-Wasabi Slaw, 77

Mignonette
Champagne, 41
Oysters, 41

Mirin
Carrot & Daikon Slaw, 191
Spicy Peanut Sauce, 63

Miso
Aioli, Charred Scallion, 118
Cream Cheese, 122

Mushroom
Salsa, Roasted, Poblano, 189

Mussels Charmoula,
148; 7, 147

Mustard *see also* Dijon
Apple Cider Ballpark, 188

Okra, Crispy Fried, 81
Okra Winfrey, 81

Onion
Bacon Fat Fried, 187
Jimmy the Greek, 56
Caramelized, 178:
Brat Michaels, 94
Just in B Bear, 68
Lamb Burger, 155
Lindsey Lowhan, 82
Senate Burger, 160
Crispy Fried, 187; 82:
Natalie Porkman, 107
White Trash Wedding, 91
Rings, 35:
Booty & Belly, 156

Orange
Fidel Castro, 212
Mr. Chow, 198
Pig Tails, 125

Oysters, 41

Pasta
Lobster Mac 'n Cheese, 32

Peach
Grilled, Salad, 128
Preserves, 138
Scissor Fight, 215

Peanut
Brown Sugar, Sauce, 185; 8, 63
Spicy, Sauce, 63; 8:
One Night in Bangkok, 63

Peanut Butter
Brown Sugar Peanut Sauce, 185
Elvis, 105
PBJ&F, 138
Spicy Peanut Sauce, 63

Peas, Wasabi
Hello Kitty Dog, 77

Pickles *see also* Cukes
Crispy Fried, 31:
Boss Hog, 84
Jesse Spano, 69
Homemade, 27; 31:
Booty & Belly, 156
Cuban, 88
Remoulade, 190
Senate Burger, 160
Sweet Potato Falafel, 139

Pico de Gallo, 114
Nacho Man Randy Savage, 114

Pineapple
Juice, Hibiscus-infused, 202
Mr. Chow, 198
Rumspringa Punch, 202

Pistachio
Syrup, 217:
Coup de Gras, 216
Scissor Fight, 215

Poblano
Beer Cheese, Roasted, 185
Salsa, Roasted Mushroom, 189
Salsa Verde, 70

Ponzu
Ginger Pork Sausage, 172
Slaw, Wasabi, 77

Pork, *see also* Bacon, Bratwurst,
Chorizo, Goetta, Ham
Apple Fennel Sausage, 173
Country Gravy, 184
Green Corn Tamale, 142
Pig Tails, 125
Substitutions, 53
Andouille Sausage, 172:
Okra Winfrey, 81
Brown Sugar Sausage, 172:
Cuban, 88
Elvis, 105
Fennel Sausage, 172:
Jersey Shore, 108
Prince Harry, 109
Ginger, Sausage, 172:
Potstickers, 122

Pork Belly, BBQ, 169:
Booty & Belly, 156
Boss Hog, 84

Pork Belly, Braised, 168; 8:
Cuban, 88
Green Corn Tamale, 142
Mc Schnitzel, 141

Vidalia Sausage, 172:
It's Brittany, 104
Just in B Bear, 68
Sarah Jessica Porker, 98

Potato, see also Fries, Grippo's
Bacon and Egg Salad, 145
Sweet Potato Falafel, 139

Potstickers, 122; 77

Poutine, 133; 7, 131, 140, 165
Dog, 92
Gravy, 184

Preserves
Cherry, 138; 140
It's Brittany, 104
PBJ&F, 138
Peach, 138

Raspberry
Kitten Fizz, 194

Relish
Apple Bacon, 95:
Brat Michaels, 94
Mc Schnitzel, 141

Black Mission Fig, 60:
Silence of the Lamb, 60

Grilled Vegetable, 93:
Madam Cleo, 93

Sweet Corn Butternut, 100:
Honey Boo Boo, 100

Sweet Corn Country, 98:
Sarah Jessica Porker, 98

Tomato, Eggplant & Onion, 108:
Jersey Shore, 108

Remoulade, 190
Jesse Spano, 69
Okra Winfrey, 81

Rum
Brown Butter-infused, 198
Cucumber Tarragon-infused, 202
Fidel Castro, 212
Homemade Spiced, 212
Mr. Chow, 198
Pooty Tang, 206
Rumspringa Punch, 202

Saffron
Mussels Charmoula, 148

Salad
Bacon and Egg, 145
Grilled Peach, 128; 93
My Wife's, 134

Salsa
Verde, 70
*Roasted Mushroom
& Poblano, 189:*
Green Corn Tamale, 142
Una Noche con Nick Lachey, 85

Salsify
Scallops, Leeks, 150

Sandwiches
Booty & Belly, 156; 27, 35, 77, 168
Lamb Burger, 155; 27
Lobster BLT, 159; 7
Mc Schnitzel, 141; 168
PBJ&F, 138; 140
Senate Burger, 160; 27
Sweet Potato Falafel, 139

Scallion
Aioli, Miso, Charred, 118
Lemony Tzatziki, 56
Pig Tails, 125
Potstickers, 122

Scallops
Leeks & Salsify, 150

Shallot
Champagne Mignonette, 41
Jam, Cranberry, 42
Marrow Butter, 179
Mussels Charmoula, 148
My Wife's Salad, 134
Tarragon Vinaigrette, 145

Shellfish
Lobster BLT, 159
Lobster Mac 'n Cheese, 32
Mussels Charmoula, 148
Oysters, 41
Scallops, Leeks & Salsify, 150

Slaw
Coleslaw, 190:
Falafel, 139
Trailer Park, 55
White Trash Wedding, 91

Apple Celery Root, 156:
Booty & Belly, 156

Carrot & Daikon, 191:
One Night in Bangkok, 63

Ponzu-Wasabi, 77:
Hello Kitty Dog, 77

Squash
Grilled Vegetable Relish, 93
Sweet Corn Butternut Relish, 100

Sriracha
Advice, 9
Braised Beef Short Ribs, 166
Brown Sugar Peanut Sauce, 185
Charmoula Sauce, 148
Mussels Charmoula, 148
Red Pepper Aioli, 99
Remoulade, 190
Spicy Peanut Sauce, 63

Substitutions, 8, 53, 194

Tamale
Green Corn, 142

Tarragon
Dressing, Buttermilk, 176
Rum, Infused, Cucumber, 202
Vinaigrette, 145

Thai, Sweet Chili Sauce
Brown Sugar Peanut Sauce, 185
Captain Jenkins, 118
One Night in Bangkok, 63
Potstickers, 122
Quick Pickled Cukes, 180
Spicy Peanut Sauce, 63

Thyme
Aioli, Garlic, 181
Braised Beef Short Ribs, 166
Braised Pork Belly, 168
Demi-glace, 182
Marrow Butter, 179
Poutine, 133
Poutine Dog, 92

Tincture
Black Pepper, 216:
Coup de Gras, 216
Chili Pepper, 205:
Ichabod Crane, 205

Tomatillo
Salsa Verde, 70

Tomato
Charmoula Sauce, 148
Demi-glace, 182
Guacamole, 176
Jimmy the Greek, 56
Lobster BLT, 159
My Wife's Salad, 134
Pico de Gallo, 114
Relish, Eggplant, Onion, 108

Roasted Mushroom
& Poblano Salsa, 189
Senate Burger, 160
Sweet Potato Falafel, 139

**Tortilla Strips,
Crispy Fried,** 186
Cabo, 101
Mexico City, 70

Truffle, Oil
Fries, 24
Lobster Mac 'n Cheese, 32

Tzatziki, Lemony, 56
Jimmy the Greek, 56

Veal
Bratwurst, 173
Demi-glace, 182

Vinegar, Apple Cider
Mustard, Ballpark, 188
Sweet Corn Country Relish, 98

Vinegar, Balsamic
Vinaigrette, 134
Glaze, 188:
It's Brittany, 104
Lindsey Lowhan, 82
PBJ&F, 138
Silence of the Lamb, 60

Vinegar, Champagne
Mignonette, 41
Roasted Mushroom
& Poblano Salsa, 189
Tarragon Vinaigrette, 145

Vodka
Kitten Fizz, 194
Limoncello, 201
Scissor Fight, 215

Walnut
Cognac, Infused, 197

Wasabi
Mayonnaise, 177

Wine, see also Champagne
Braised Beef Short Ribs, 166
Demi-glace, 182
Emulsion, Sauternes and Fig, 217
Scissor Fight, 215
Shallot Cranberry Jam, 42

Yogurt
Lemony Tzatziki, 56
Cilantro, 188:
Bollywood, 117
Sweet Potato Falafel, 139